Ancien

Charles Kovacs

Ancient Greece

Waldorf Education Resources

Floris Books

Edited by Peter Snow
First published in volume form in 2004

© 2004 Estate of Charles Kovacs
The author has asserted his right under the
Copyright, Design and Patents Act 1988
to be identified as the Author of this Work.

British Library CIP Data available

ISBN 0-86315-396-8

Printed in Great Britain
by Cromwell Press, Trowbridge

Contents

The Twelve Labours of Heracles

Theseus

Greek History

Preface

Charles Kovacs was a teacher at the Rudolf Steiner School in Edinburgh for many years. The Waldorf/Steiner schools sprang from the pedagogical ideas and insights of the Austrian philosopher Rudolf Steiner (1864–1925). The curriculum aims to awaken much more than merely the intellectual development—it seeks to educate the whole being of the growing child, that each may develop their full human and spiritual potential.

During his time as a class teacher Charles Kovacs wrote his extensive main lesson notes day by day from Class 1 to 8 to help colleagues in search of suitable source material. Since then the texts have been used and appreciated by teachers in Edinburgh for many years.

This book represents the way in which one teacher taught a particular group of children. Other teachers will find their own way of presenting the material, but the content of the stories, the narrative style and the mood Kovacs tried to create provides valuable source material, particularly for a teacher new to the subject.

Greek Mythology

1. The Red Flower of the Gods

The Greeks lived in a country called Greece which is part of the continent of Europe. Greece is not a large country; it is a peninsula, which means it is surrounded on three sides by the sea. Around its coasts lie many islands both large and small. The winter is short and wet, and snow is rare, while the summer is long, dry and often very hot. While the stories about ancient India, Persia, Babylon and Egypt happened a very long time ago, the stories in this book are only about three thousand years old. King Arthur lived about a thousand years ago, Christ lived on earth a thousand years before that, and if we go back another thousand years we come to the time of ancient Greece.

The people of Greece loved stories about gods and heroes. They did not have books, but there were men who travelled from village to village telling the people such stories. In the evening, when the sun sank into the glittering blue sea, the people stopped work. The men came back from the fields, the fishermen came from the shore, the women came from their little houses, the children stopped playing, and they all gathered in the market square and sat down around the story-teller. He did not tell his stories as I tell them to you now. He had a harp and he told his tales, which were in verse, as if he was singing a song.

And one of these stories or songs went like this: High are the mountains you see from your village, but far in the north of Greece there towers a mountain whose snow-covered peak reaches into the clouds. It is called Mount Olympus. And the heights of Olympus are the home of the gods. There the Olympians live. They are the immortals who never die, who never grow old.

And their ruler is mighty Zeus, his long hair falls to his broad shoulders; a full beard frames his face. In his hands he holds thunderbolts, and at his feet is perched the eagle, his messenger.

Great was Zeus, the King of the Gods, but he and the other gods did not always rule the world. A race of wild giants, called Titans, had been masters of the world until Zeus and his companions defeated them in a terrible battle. And the defeated Titans were banished to caves deep in the earth, to be imprisoned forever.

But two of the wisest Titans, Prometheus and his brother Epimetheus, had helped Zeus in the battle. They knew that the wild, savage ways of the giants had to come to an end, and they were not imprisoned with their fellow Titans.

At that time, life on earth was difficult. There were many wild animals around but people had no weapons to fight them with and lived in fear and dread. However these people were also wild and lawless and Zeus often thought the best thing to do would be to destroy them all. But Prometheus took a liking to these uncivilized people and he often wondered how he could help them to master the animals they were so afraid of.

But Zeus, the King of the Gods, had no wish to see the human race become more powerful. One day, however, Prometheus decided he would help the human race whether Zeus liked it or not. And the Titan thought that the red flower of the gods was what would help man most. What was the red flower? It was fire. Today we take fire for granted. We use it to cook our food, to light our houses at night and to keep us warm. But in those days people ate their food raw and huddled together in the cold and dark for warmth and protection from the wild beasts. Prometheus also knew that animals are afraid of fire. If, for instance, you were in the wilds at night and you made a blazing fire, no wild animals would come near you.

Now, the ancient Greeks believed the sun was a fiery chariot that the Sun God Helios drove across the sky each day. Prometheus climbed a high mountain and as Helios' chariot passed by he held out a long, dry stalk of the fennel plant and it soon began to smoulder. Carrying the smouldering stem, Prometheus hurried down to bring his gift to the human race. People looked on with awe and wonder when, from tiny sparks, he kindled a roaring fire. Then Prometheus told them that the red flower would not only keep the wild beasts away but would also keep them warm and cook their food. The Titan also explained that they could use fire to make metal from the earth into weapons sharper and more deadly than any animal's claws.

Once the human race received the gift of fire, mankind began to master the forces of nature and make weapons and tools. However, it was not long before Zeus found out that Prometheus had disobeyed him by bringing the red flower to mankind. The King of the Gods was very angry. "He has stolen the fire from us but he shall not go unpunished," Zeus cried.

2. Pandora's Box

Zeus called his two servants Cratos and Bia (which means Strength and Force), and said: "Take the disobedient Titan far away to the east. Take him to the towering mountains called Caucasus and chain him to a rock so that he cannot move. He shall not die, but he shall remain bound to the rock forever. I, Zeus, King of the Gods swear it." Cratos and Bia dragged the struggling Prometheus to the Caucasus mountains and chained him to a steep cliff above a deep chasm. Prometheus was left alone hanging in chains from the rock as punishment for bringing fire to humanity. In the summer the sun scorched his skin and rain fell on him, in the winter he shivered in the cold winds and snow covered his limbs. But after many, many years a great hero came to the rock where he was chained and set him free. This hero's name was Heracles and his many great deeds are told later (pp. 77ff).

In the meantime, the ancient Greeks became very powerful. They learnt to watch the movement of the stars; to make chariots and ships and metal weapons and tools. In the Greek stories, this time is called the Golden Age for people were never sick; they lived to a very old age and died peacefully. They had no worries and no sorrows, no aches or pains.

Prometheus had a brother called Epimetheus. Now Prometheus had often warned his brother about one thing. He said: "If Zeus sends you a gift, do not take it, you must send it back." Not long after Prometheus was taken to the Caucasus, Epimetheus received a visit from the god Hermes. Hermes was both the messenger of the gods and the protector of merchants and sailors. He had wings on his cap and heels, and could fly faster than lightning. But Hermes did not come alone: he brought with him a beautiful young woman and carried a lovely little box. The Messenger God said to Epimetheus: "This is Pandora, which means One-Who-Has-All-The-Gifts, for she is

not only beautiful but also gentle and clever. Zeus has sent her
to you so you will not be lonely now that Prometheus has gone.
Zeus also sends you this box, but you can only enjoy it by looking at it from the outside. It must never be opened."

Pandora was so beautiful that Epimetheus decided to forget
his brother's warning. He accepted both gifts: the girl and the
box. For a time all went well and it seemed that Prometheus'
warning had been unnecessary. But one day when Pandora was
at home alone she looked at the lovely box that Hermes had left
and wondered what might be inside it. In the end her curiosity
got the better of her and she lifted the lid.

As soon as the lid was open, it was as if she had taken the
cover off a beehive: hundreds and hundreds of little winged
creatures came out. They flew through the house and out of the
windows and spread in all directions. But they were not bees, or
butterflies or birds; they were nothing other than hundreds of
illnesses and worries. And from that moment the Golden Age
came to an end for illness, worry and trouble had come to
mankind.

When Pandora saw all the strange creatures fly out she
quickly shut the box. But it was too late for only one little
winged creature remained inside. This was the only good being
in the box and it pleaded and pleaded to be let out. In the end
Pandora opened the lid again and out came something that was
like a great shining white butterfly, and that was Hope. And so,
when we are sick or have worries, it is Hope that can help us to
overcome our difficulties.

3. An Apple for Aphrodite

In the olden days, story-tellers travelled from village to village singing songs based on the ancient stories. The most famous of them was Homer. He was blind, but he could make up poems and speak and sing them like no one else. And long after he died, other story-tellers who had learnt songs from him repeated them again and again, for people loved to hear them. Later on when there were books and writing, the songs of blind Homer were written down and people who have learnt the Greek language can still read them today in Homer's own words.

This is one of the stories that Homer told: The most beautiful young woman that ever lived on earth was Helen, the daughter of the King of Sparta, a city famous in the history of Greece. When Helen reached the age of marriage, mighty kings came from every part of Greece to court her. Now in those days young women, even kings' daughters, did not choose their own husbands; it was up to the father to decide who should become his son-in-law.

But it was very difficult for the King of Sparta to make a decision. If he chose one suitor, no matter which, the others would become his enemies and terrible strife and bloodshed would follow. Now, among the kings there was one named Odysseus whose kingdom was a little island called Ithaca. Though he was only a minor king, no man in Greece was wiser or more clever. And Odysseus told Helen's father: "Call the suitors together and tell them that you will not make any decision unless they all swear by Zeus that they will protect and help Helen's future husband, whoever that may be."

The King of Sparta chose a tall, strong, fair-haired and blue-eyed warrior-king called Menelaus to be Helen's husband. After they were married, the couple made their home in Sparta and eventually Menelaus became king. The other suitors kept their promise and nobody tried to fight the lucky Menelaus. Each returned to his own kingdom and found a good wife for himself. Clever Odysseus, the King of Ithaca, also went home and got married.

But Menelaus, being fond of war, was often away from home, seeking fame as a warrior, and beautiful Helen was left alone with her servants in Sparta. One day while Menelaus was away a ship arrived in Sparta carrying visitors from the city of Troy.

Troy, however, was not a Greek city. It lay across the sea from Greece on the coast of Asia in the country now called Turkey. And the people who came from the rich and powerful city of Troy were Trojans, not Greeks. The King of Troy had several sons and he loved his boys and was proud of them. But he feared a dark prophecy about one of his sons — the one called Paris. Before the child was born, his mother, the queen, had a strange dream that she was giving birth to a burning torch which set the whole city of Troy ablaze and burnt it to ashes.

The prince grew up to be a handsome young man. But the king was so afraid of his wife's dream that for a time Paris was not allowed to stay in Troy. He was sent outside the city walls to live as a shepherd in the hills.

One day when Paris was herding his sheep something happened to him that had not happened to any other man: he had to be the judge in a quarrel between three goddesses. Three women stood on the hillside before him, each more wonderful than any earthly woman could be. The first was tall and stately. She wore a cloak of royal purple and said: "I am Hera, the wife of Zeus, the Queen of the Gods." The second wore armour and a helmet. She carried a spear like a warrior, but her face shone with beauty and it seemed as if all the knowledge in the world was in her glance. "I am Pallas Athene, the Goddess of Wisdom," she said. The third was dressed in white. Her eyes were as blue as the sea, her hair was like ripe corn and she was as lovely as a rose in the morning dew. She said: "I am Aphrodite, the Goddess of Love, and we have chosen you, Paris, to decide which of us is the most beautiful."

Poor Paris! How could he, a mortal man, judge immortals? Hera promised him power and riches if he chose her as the most beautiful, Pallas Athene promised him fame and wisdom, but Aphrodite smiled at him and said: "I will give you the most beautiful woman on earth to be your wife, if you decide for me." Then Hera gave Paris a golden apple and said: "You must give this apple to the goddess you think is the most beautiful." Dazzled by the charms of Aphrodite and beguiled by her promise, Paris held out the apple to the Goddess of Love. The other goddesses turned their backs and went away. Aphrodite repeated her promise then she too left, and Paris was alone.

Later he returned to his father's city and it seemed that his mother's dream had been forgotten. And it was Paris, the Prince of Troy, who came with a ship and many warriors to visit Sparta when Helen's husband was away.

4. Helen's Abduction

Paris sailed to Sparta in a ship with many men aboard. King Menelaus was away but Helen received the visitors with royal hospitality, and they were served with choice food and drinks. But Paris hardly noticed the food placed before him; he had eyes only for his beautiful hostess. It seemed to him that in Helen he saw an earthly image of Aphrodite. And had the goddess not promised him the most beautiful woman on earth? Forgetting all the rules of decency and honesty, Paris called his warriors together and, with promises of rich plunder, he persuaded them to help him. They stormed the palace, seized the treasures of King Menelaus, and carried off the beautiful Helen to their ship. Then they sailed away to Troy. And through the power of Aphrodite, the Goddess of Love, Helen came to like the handsome Paris and in the end forgot her husband, Menelaus.

But Paris had broken the sacred laws of hospitality. Not only was Menelaus raging with fury when he returned; all Greeks felt they had been insulted by the impertinence of the Trojan prince. Moreover, the kings who had promised to stand by Helen's husband Menelaus were bound by their oath to help him. So Menelaus sent his messengers out calling on his friends to send ships and warriors to sail against Troy. Soon there was a mighty fleet ready to cross the sea and bring Helen back to Sparta.

But two warriors did not want to join the fighting. One was Odysseus who had married a noble lady called Penelope. She had just had a baby and Odysseus had no wish to leave his wife and young son to fight for Menelaus in a war that might go on for years. When the messenger came Odysseus pretended he had gone mad. He hitched an ox and an ass to a plough and started ploughing a field, but instead of sowing seed he scattered salt in the furrows. The messenger looked at this strange behaviour for a while, then he went quietly to the palace and found Odysseus' son asleep in his cot. He took him out, carried him to the field and put him on the ground in the path of the plough. When Odysseus came near he stopped the ox and ass and carried the baby out of the way. Then the messenger laughed aloud and said to Odysseus: "If you are sane enough to rescue your child, then you are also sane enough to fight by the side of Menelaus." And so wily Odysseus had to give up his pretence and come along.

The other warrior who would not join the great fleet of the Greeks was called Achilles. He was too young to have been one of Helen's suitors so he had not made a promise to help Menelaus. But the Greeks wanted the young Achilles because a soothsayer, a priest who could foresee the future, had said that without him they could not win the war against Troy. Why was he so necessary for a Greek victory? Prince Achilles was the son of a king and the Sea Goddess Thetis. Being a goddess, Thetis was immortal, but her son, Achilles, having a human father, was mortal; he would die like other men. Now, when Achilles was a baby his mother decided to make her son invulnerable so that no weapon could harm him. So, one night, when her husband was asleep, she took the child and held him by one heel over a fire which she had prepared in a special way. The magic fire made Achilles' skin invulnerable; no spear or sword could pierce it.★

But while she was doing this her husband woke up and wondered where his wife was. The king went looking for her and to his horror found her holding their son over the fire. With a cry of horror he rushed in, tore the child from her hands and cursed her. So insulted was the Goddess of the Sea that she did not explain what she had been doing. She simply walked out and went back to the depths of the ocean. But the child, Achilles, had become invulnerable — all except for the heel where Thetis had held him. Yet Thetis still feared for her son because he remained vulnerable in this one spot. And when she learnt that

★ According to another tradition, Thetis dipped the infant Achilles in the River Styx, (one of the rivers of the Underworld) holding him by the heel to do so. This rendered the child invulnerable to all harm, except in the heel. - P.S.

the Greeks wanted Achilles to go and fight, she left her kingdom beneath the waves and secretly entered her husband's palace. Thetis found Achilles and told him that, for her sake, he must come with her and do as she said. So Achilles went away with his mother. Thetis dressed him up as a girl, and brought him to a king to be a servant for the king's daughter. And for a time, Achilles lived as a servant girl in the palace of that king.

But the soothsayer who had told the Greeks they needed Achilles for victory, predicted that he would be found dressed as a girl in the palace of a king. From the description the priest gave, the Greeks worked out where Achilles was hiding and wily Odysseus and a companion were sent to fetch him. They went to the palace and told the king why they had come. The king said that if there was a man among his daughter's servants they must find him themselves. Odysseus and his companion looked at the servants but the young Achilles looked so much like a girl that they could not detect him. Then Odysseus thought of a clever plan. He had a spear and shield brought into the hall. Then, without warning, his companion outside suddenly blew a war trumpet. The girls scattered in all directions but Achilles seized the spear and shield and stood, ready to fight.

Achilles had been unmasked, but the young prince was tired of living as a girl for he loved war and fighting and had only disguised himself for his mother's sake. Since the disguise had failed he was pleased to go with Odysseus and join the Greeks in their fight against the Trojans. And so a great fleet of a thousand ships carrying a huge army and many heroes like Menelaus, Achilles and Odysseus, set out to sail across the sea to Troy.

5. The Battle for Troy

Paris had broken the laws of hospitality in Sparta. He had been received kindly as a guest yet he had rewarded this kindness by stealing King Menelaus' wife and treasure. Do not think that his father, the King of Troy, or his brothers, or the people of Troy approved of what Paris had done. They knew it was wrong to steal a man's wife. And it is quite possible that the Trojans would have sent Helen back to her husband, whether Paris liked it or not. But the Greeks had sent messengers demanding that Helen and the treasure be given back. The messengers threatened the Trojans and told the King of Troy: "You Trojan people are nothing but thieves. If you don't give back what you have stolen, and more gold besides as punishment for Paris' foul deed, you shall feel the whole weight of Greece. We will make you crawl in the dust and beg for mercy." But the Trojans were a proud and brave people. They would not be insulted or give in to threats. So they refused to give Helen or the treasure back and the messengers returned to Greece with the news that the Trojans were prepared to fight.

So the mighty Greek fleet crossed the sea to Troy. The splendid city, which was protected by high and thick walls, lay inland from the coast. The Greek ships were beached and thousands of warriors poured ashore to begin building a great camp. They dug up the earth and made rough huts for themselves and bigger houses for the kings. They also made earth walls to protect their camp which soon grew to be like a huge city.

They were still hard at work when the gates in the walls of Troy opened and out poured Trojan warriors led by the greatest hero of Troy, Paris' brother Hector. Hector ordered the Trojans to attack. The Greeks were taken by surprise and many were killed. But they soon recovered; they threw down their spades and shovels, picked up their weapons and rushed into the fight.

And when Achilles began to strike his enemies down right and left, the Trojans turned and fled back behind the walls of Troy.

That was the first encounter, and from then on there was fighting every day. Sometimes the Trojans won and the Greeks retreated. Sometimes the Greeks gained the upper hand and chased the fleeing Trojans right to the gates of Troy. Yet none of these battles brought final victory.

But it was not only a war between the Greek and Trojan people; the gods also took sides. Hera, the wife of Zeus, and Pallas Athene helped the Greeks, but Aphrodite, the Goddess of Love, helped the Trojans. In one battle, Menelaus caught sight of Paris among the Trojans. Roaring with rage, he attacked the man who had stolen his wife. Menelaus threw his spear with such force that it went right through Paris's shield and breast-plate and wounded him badly. But when Menelaus drew his sword to kill him, Aphrodite, who had watched the fight invisibly, quickly threw her veil over Paris, and Menelaus could no longer see his enemy. Paris had become invisible and the Goddess of Love took her wounded favourite safely away from the battle and back behind the sheltering walls of Troy.

Another god also helped the Trojans. He was called Apollo, the God of the Sun Rays. He was the divine marksman with bow and arrow; no arrow sent from his shining bow ever missed, just as the sun's rays come straight from the sun to earth. Now, some distance from the Greek camp stood a temple to Apollo where a priest made daily sacrifices to the god and sang hymns in his praise. The priest had a beautiful daughter who helped with the service. When the Greeks saw the girl, they thought she was so beautiful that she would make a wonderful servant for their heroes and kings, so they broke into the temple and dragged her away. The old priest pleaded with them in vain and, after his daughter was taken away, he prayed to Apollo for revenge. From that time Apollo, the god who never misses his mark, became an enemy of the Greeks.

Through this deed other misfortunes befell the Greeks. The kings quarrelled about whose servant the captured girl should be. When, in the end, she was given to a king who was Menelaus's brother, young Achilles, who wanted the girl himself, was so angry that he refused to fight any more. While the battles went on, day after day, Achilles sat in his house and sulked. But then something happened that changed his mind. With Achilles out of the way, Hector, the older brother of Paris and the greatest hero among the Trojans, came upon the Greeks like a raging torrent.

Neither Menelaus nor Odysseus could stand up to Hector, and every day countless Greeks fell to his sword. One day Hector struck down Patroclus, a Greek warrior who was Achilles' friend. When Achilles heard of the death, a wild anger came over him. He left his hut and joined the battle again, his heart set on revenge.

When Achilles returned to the battle, Hector was inside Troy, resting from hours of fighting. But when he learnt that Achilles was slaying Trojans as a lion would slay sheep, he called for his weapons and shield. Hector's wife wept bitter tears. She pleaded with him not to fight the terrible Achilles, who was invulnerable. She brought Hector's little son and cried: "Shall our child be left without father?" But Hector answered: "I would be without honour if I were to hide behind walls for fear of Achilles. Shall I, a prince of Troy, show less courage than the common soldiers, the Trojans who are battling against him now?" So Hector embraced his wife and went to meet Achilles.

6. The Great Wooden Horse

Achilles, in his fury to avenge the death of Patroclus, had driven the Trojans right back to the walls of Troy, and his path was strewn with the dead and wounded that had fallen to his fearful strength. And when Hector saw Achilles' spear and sword stained with the blood of his victims, his heart was filled with fear and he turned to flee. But Achilles had seen him and was after him in a flash. Hector ran along the walls of Troy as fast as he could but Achilles was faster and started to catch up.

At that moment on the heights of Olympus, Zeus, the far-seeing King of the Gods, took a pair of scales in his hand. On one side he put a weight with Hector's name on it, and on the other, an equal weight with Achilles' name on it. The side with Hector's name on it went down and then all the gods knew that Hector was doomed.

After Achilles had chased Hector around the walls of Troy four times, Hector turned and stood fast. He lifted his spear and threw it with all his might at Achilles. But Achilles held up his shield and the spear bounced off and fell to the ground. Now Achilles threw his own spear so swiftly and cunningly that Hector could not catch it on his shield, and it found a gap in the Trojan's armour between his breast-plate and shoulder-plate. With blood spurting from the deadly wound Hector fell to the ground. As Achilles bent over his fallen foe, Hector spoke his last words: "Do not rejoice over your victory, Achilles. It will not be long before you follow me to the dark land of the dead." Then Hector's spirit left his body.

Achilles ordered the soldiers to bring his chariot and horses. He tied ropes to Hector's ankles, fastened the ropes to the back of the chariot and drove it round the walls of Troy, dragging the body through the dust. The Trojans watching from the top of the walls cried with grief over the fall of Hector, the noble prince of Troy.

Now, Apollo, the god whose arrows never missed their

mark, had been offended by the Greeks when they took away
the priest's daughter to be a slave. Since then they had learnt to
fear Apollo's anger. Even though they had returned the girl to
her father, the god had not forgiven them for breaking into his
holy temple. One day Apollo looked down from the heights of
Olympus and saw the battles raging outside Troy. He saw
Achilles driving the Trojans before him as the wind drives leaves
in the autumn, for no one could stand against the invulnerable
warrior. Then Apollo made a decision. He picked up his bow
and arrows, hid himself in a cloud of mist and came down from
Olympus to the battlefield.

He called out to Achilles: "Let the Trojans be. Make an end
of the slaughter, Achilles. If you do not it will not be a man but
one of the immortals who will destroy you." Achilles knew it
was a god who spoke from the cloud, but he was too proud to
heed the warning, and he answered: "Neither mortal man nor
immortal god shall make me cease fighting." Then Apollo put
an arrow to his bowstring, took aim, and sent his shaft into
Achilles' heel, the only place where he could be wounded.
Achilles felt a stinging pain from his heel right up to his heart,
and he knew the end was coming. But with his last strength he
drew the arrow from the wound and used it to slay the Trojans
around him. Then he sank to the ground and died.

When Apollo returned to Olympus Aphrodite praised him
for what he had done, but Hera and Pallas Athene were angry.
And down on earth, now that the invulnerable Achilles and the
brave Hector had gone, the Greeks and Trojans were equal in
strength. Even Paris, who had caused the war by taking Helen
from her husband, was struck by an arrow and died of his
wound. But neither side could gain victory and the battles and
bloodshed had gone on for nine years.

Then, in the tenth year of the war, the goddess Pallas Athene
inspired Prylis, one of the Greek warriors, to say to Menelaus
and the other kings: "For many years we have battled against the
Trojans. Countless brave men have lost their lives, and we are as
far from victory as ever. Surely you can all see that by force of
arms alone we cannot win. We must use cunning, we must
deceive the Trojans if we want to end the war and return to our

homes. Now listen to my plan. We shall make an enormous wooden horse but its belly will be hollow. Inside the belly we will hide many brave warriors. The others will burn our camp and sail away, but just far enough so the ships can no longer be seen from Troy. One of us, however, must stay behind to tell the Trojans we have given up the struggle and gone back to Greece. That soldier must persuade them to pull the great wooden horse into Troy. But, at night, when the Trojans have celebrated the end of the war and are asleep, our warriors will come out of the horse, our ships will come back in the darkness, and together we will destroy the city with fire and sword."

There were some Greeks who said it was not worthy of brave warriors to use such cunning, but most of them were longing to return to their homes and in the end they all agreed. And so, as the Trojans watched from the walls of their city, they saw, to their astonishment, the Greeks making an enormous wooden horse. But what the Trojans did not see was that at night armed men went inside the belly of the horse through a door so cleverly made that no one could see it from the outside. Then the Trojans saw the Greeks set fire to their camp, board their ships and sail away to disappear over the horizon.

Victorious, the Trojans came out of the city. Sitting by the great horse they found a Greek who begged them for mercy. He explained that the Greeks had tired of fighting and had made the horse in honour of Pallas Athene so that she would guide them home safely across the sea. "Why have you not gone with them?" asked the Trojans. The soldier answered: "Because they wanted to make a human sacrifice to the gods and I was the one chosen to be killed at the altar. But I fled and hid myself until they had gone."

The Trojans were so pleased with the news that the Greeks had left that they spared the man's life. But then the Greek soldier said: "They made the wooden horse too big to go through the gates in the walls of Troy. For if you were to take it inside, Pallas Athene would give her protection to you instead of the Greeks." Of course when they heard that, the Trojans wanted to bring the horse into the city. So they tore down part of the wall and began to drag the great horse through the breach into the city.

7. Odysseus the Wanderer

The Trojans believed the Greeks had sailed away for good. And if, as the soldier had said, the wooden horse would bring the protection of the goddess Pallas Athene, then they wanted the horse inside their city. As there were no longer any enemies to fear, the Trojans did not care if they knocked down part of the wall to get it through. They put wheels on the horse's feet, fastened ropes to its neck and, pulled by many strong men, the huge horse rolled into Troy.

They left it standing in a big square while the whole city gave itself up to feasting and celebrating. There was dancing and singing, cups were filled with wine and drained to the last drop. But at midnight the Trojans grew tired, and it was not long before they were all fast asleep. Silently, the trap door in the horse's belly opened, and a rope ladder was let down. The Greeks drew their swords and scattered through the city. At the same time the Greek fleet returned in the darkness, and thousands of warriors poured into the doomed city through the hole in the wall.

The Trojans, dazed with sleep and wine, were taken by surprise and slaughtered. Burning torches were tossed into their homes and soon whole streets were ablaze. The Greeks raged through the city like tigers, killing the helpless Trojans without mercy, and sparing only those women and children who might be useful as slaves. And from the palaces and temples they took all the silver and gold they could find.

Helen trembled and shivered with fear in the royal palace: she expected Menelaus, the husband she had left behind, to kill her. And when Menelaus stormed in, his sword stained with the blood of the Trojans, she sank to her knees awaiting her death. But Aphrodite, the Goddess of Love, stood invisibly beside her and made her look lovelier than ever. Even Menelaus could not resist her beauty, his sword fell from his hand, and he forgave her and took her in his arms.

By now, all of Troy was burning. The Greeks, carrying their plunder and driving the captured women and children before them, left the doomed city and the piles of dead Trojans lying in the streets. The whole city went up in flames and the fire and smoke could be seen miles away.

When daylight came, the once splendid city of Troy was nothing but rubble and ashes. And the Greeks, now that victory was theirs, and Menelaus had his wife back, boarded their ships, longing to return to the homes they had not seen for ten long years.

But their return voyage was not as quick or as smooth as their passage to Troy had been. It was not long before the Greeks ran into a great storm which scattered the fleet. Then each little group of ships had to make its own way home. But none of the other Greeks had as many terrible adventures or encountered as many hardships and dangers as Odysseus, the wise and cunning king of Ithaca.

Odysseus had seven ships under his command. For nine days the winds roared and waves as big as mountains tossed the boats about as if they were nutshells. At long last the sea grew calm. The sailors did not know where the storm had blown them and when they saw an island they made for it, glad to cast anchor after all they had gone through. Happily the sea-battered sailors stepped ashore on to green meadows. Then Odysseus chose twelve men to accompany him exploring the island. The others were told to wait on the shore until he returned.

Soon the explorers came to an enormous cave in the side of a mountain. When they went into the cave they saw that the walls were lined with pens full of sheep. They also saw buckets of milk and great slabs of cheese, so Odysseus and his friends sat down and helped themselves while they waited for the owner to return.

At last he came. But what a shock the Greeks got when they saw that the owner of the cave was a Cyclops. In fact, as they would discover, the whole island was inhabited by such creatures. But what was a Cyclops? Odysseus and his companions saw a giant, with legs as thick as the trunks of old oak trees and hands that could have played ball with blocks of granite. But what terrified them most was that instead of having two eyes, the giant had one single eye in the middle of his forehead. When the one-eyed giant came into the cave, Odysseus and his companions rushed into a dark corner to hide. But they were even more afraid when they saw the Cyclops close the entrance to the cave with an enormous rock which even fifty men could not have moved. The Cyclops sat down, then looked round and saw the men huddling in a corner. "And who might you be?" he growled. "We are shipwrecked sailors," answered Odysseus. "We pray for your hospitality in the name of Zeus who has ruled that one must give help to strangers." "Hospitality, indeed," laughed the Cyclops. He put out his huge hands, grabbed two of the men and threw them to the ground with such force that they died instantly. To the horror of Odysseus and his remaining companions the giant threw the bodies into a great cauldron, cooked them over a fire and ate them. Then he lay down, closed his one big eye and went to sleep.

8. No One and the Cyclops

The one-eyed giant, the Cyclops, was asleep. Odysseus could have plunged his sword into the monster's belly but he and his companions could never have moved the enormous rock from the entrance of the cave. Their only hope was to get away when the cave was open. In the morning the giant woke up and grabbed two more men. After he had eaten them for breakfast, he rolled the rock away to let his sheep out to graze in the fields. Then the Cyclops pushed the rock back and the Greeks were trapped again. However, during the day, Odysseus, cunning as ever, thought of a way to deal with the one-eyed giant.

In the evening the Cyclops came home with his sheep. He opened the cave to let the sheep in and pushed the heavy rock back in place. Once again he killed two men for his loathsome evening meal. When he had finished eating, Odysseus approached him with a gift. Odysseus had taken a wine-filled flask made of goat skin with him when he set out to explore the island, and it was this he now offered the Cyclops. Of course a Cyclops would never say "thank you" but, after drinking some of the wine, he got friendly enough to ask: "What is your name!" And the wily Odysseus answered: "I am called No One." "Well," said the Cyclops, "as a reward for this gift of wine, my dear No One, you will be the last I eat."

Having eaten and drunk the strong wine, the Cyclops was soon drowsy and fell asleep. But as soon as the monster was snoring, Odysseus and his men got busy. At the back of the cave they found an enormous club that belonged to the Cyclops. They took the weapon, sharpened one end, and placed it in the giant's fire until it was glowing hot. Together they carried the club to the Cyclops' head, and then, with one great heave, rammed it into the eye on his forehead. Roaring and howling the Cyclops leapt up and tried to catch his enemies. But now he was blind and Odysseus and his companions darted this way and that and escaped his clutches.

But the Cyclops made such a noise that the other giants heard it and hurried to the cave. It was still blocked with the rock, so they could not see what was going on inside. They called out: "What is the matter with you, in there? Why are you shouting?" And the Cyclops in the cave answered: "I shout because No One has hurt me." When the other Cyclops heard this, they said: "He must be mad, he shouts for no reason. No one has done anything to him." And they left.

When the Cyclops in the cave found he could not catch his enemies he tried something else. He rolled the rock from the entrance and sat down by the opening, hoping they would try to escape. But Odysseus had other plans. In the morning when the sheep were let out of their pens to graze, Odysseus tied three rams together so that they could only walk side by side. Then one man hid under the middle ram and, by clinging on to the animal's woolly belly, he was carried outside. The Cyclops, guarding the entrance, touched the animals as they passed, but he never thought of reaching under them. So, carried under the bellies of the sheep, the Greeks escaped from the cave without the blind Cyclops knowing.

Once they were all safely outside, they celebrated and hurried to join their friends on the coast. Wasting no time the Greeks boarded their ships but the Cyclops had heard their voices and came lumbering after them. But the blind giant could only move slowly and the ships had sailed away by the time he got to the coast. Raging, he hurled rocks after them, but the Greeks only laughed as they sailed out to sea.

The next island they reached was the home of the Wind God, Aeolus. He was friendly to the seafarers and gave Odysseus a bag with all the winds in it. The Wind God said: "Keep this bag well closed. If you need some wind to blow into your sails, just open the bag a little." But when the ships were at sea again and Odysseus was asleep, some of the sailors wondered what treasure was hidden in the bag. They opened it wide and out flew all the winds. A raging tempest broke out and in that terrible storm only Odysseus' ship remained afloat. All the others sank and the sailors drowned.

The surviving ship with Odysseus and his crew aboard sailed

on until they came to another island. They went ashore for they were running out of food and in the distance saw smoke rising from a building. Odysseus decided to send some of his men to explore the island. Under the leadership of a man called Eurylochus, the party set out and found the building was a beautiful palace. To their amazement they saw that the gardens around the palace were full of wild animals — lions, tigers and wolves — which were as tame as dogs and wagged their tails in a strangely gentle and friendly manner.

Eurylochus thought there must be something wrong with lions that behaved like dogs, and he told his men to find out who lived in the palace. Eurylochus stayed outside and peeped through a window to see what would happen. Now the palace was the home of a beautiful sorceress, a queen who possessed great powers of magic. Her name was Circe, and when the sailors went inside, the fair queen Circe and her maidens made them welcome. Dishes of lovely food were put before them and Eurylochus began to feel sorry he had not joined the feast. But there were queer concoctions in the food and drink the sailors were enjoying. Anybody who ate or drank the food and wine could be changed by Circe into any animal she chose. And as soon as the sailors swallowed some of the food, Queen Circe waved her magic wand over them and they turned into swine. The poor pigs grunted and squealed but Circe and her maidens only laughed and drove them into the pigsties. Eurylochus was horrified. He realized that the lions and tigers were also really human beings and he ran back to tell Odysseus what had happened.

9. Circe the Sorceress

When Eurylochus, the leader of the party that Circe had changed into pigs, reached Odysseus he was so frightened he could hardly speak. When he finally told his story, Odysseus took his sword and set out alone to rescue his men and punish Circe. He had only gone a short distance when a shining figure with wings on his heels appeared before him. It was Hermes, and the Messenger of the Gods said to Odysseus: "On your own you will not be able to help your companions. Circe has great powers and she can turn you into a beast too. But I have been sent to help you. Take this plant I have brought for you. It will protect you against her magic." It was a little plant with a white flower. Then Hermes disappeared and Odysseus walked on towards the palace.

Queen Circe welcomed the Greek in the same friendly way that she had received his companions. Odysseus was offered a cup of sweet, sparkling wine but he had hardly put the cup down when Circe lifted her wand and cried: "Go down on all fours, you pig!" However to her amazement and terror Odysseus did not change into a pig. He was still a man, a very angry man. As he drew his sword Circe fell to her knees and cried out: "You must be Odysseus for it has been foretold that, of all men, only Odysseus will resist my magic powers. O, have mercy, great hero, and spare my life!"

But Odysseus answered: "You will die this very moment unless you swear a sacred oath that you will not harm me. You must also turn my friends and the other poor creatures in your garden into men again!" Circe swore to do as Odysseus had asked her. The poor, grunting pigs, the lions and tigers and other animals, were brought in and Circe magically turned them all into men again. Odysseus' men and the others who had been changed from animals into human beings again, thanked him warmly.

But Circe did more than this: to make up for the suffering she had caused she invited Odysseus and his men to be her guests for as long as they liked. The sailors waiting on the coast were summoned to the palace, and after all the hardships they had gone through, the seafarers now enjoyed every comfort they would wish for. Life was so pleasant on the island that a whole year went by before they remembered their homes and families and decided to sail away.

Then Circe said to Odysseus: "I must not try and keep you. But if you want to reach home safely you must first seek the advice of the dead." "The advice of the dead?" asked Odysseus astonished. "Yes," replied Circe. "There are many dangers ahead, but the souls of the dead know them and can tell you how to protect yourself." Then Circe said: "After many days sailing you will come to an island where tall poplars grow. On that island you will find a great cleft, a huge ravine in the earth, which is the entrance to the Underworld — the land of the dead. There you must make a sacrifice of honey, flour, milk and wine. Then, if you pray, the souls of the dead will come. But you must wait for one, a wise priest whom you last saw alive before the walls of Troy. His name was Tiresias and his soul will tell you what is in store for you."

So Odysseus followed the advice of the wise queen. He and his companions said farewell to Circe who had become a true friend to them, and set sail. A strong north wind carried the ship to the island of poplars and they soon found the great gap in the earth which was the entrance to the Underworld.

When Odysseus had made his offering many souls of the dead appeared. They seemed like shadows; some were unknown to Odysseus but others he recognized. The soul of Achilles, the great hero of the Trojan War, appeared and Odysseus called out: "Achilles, my dear comrade, are you honoured for your great deeds in the land of the dead?" Achilles answered: "Yes, great honour is given to me, but I would rather be the poorest slave among living people than a lord and king among the dead." So spoke Achilles and went away.

Many other souls appeared: Greeks and Trojans who had died in the fighting at Troy and heroes who had lived and died long before Odysseus was born. Then the soul of the priest Tiresias came and said: "Odysseus, your journey will take you to an island where the Oxen of the Sun God are grazing. Do not touch them or you will lose your ship and your friends. Even if you escape, it will take many more years until you reach Ithaca, your home. Even then you will have to overcome many enemies and dangers before the gods will give you peace and comfort."

Having heard the priest's warning, Odysseus and his men sailed away from the strange island where the poplars grew.

10. The Sirens' Song

Soon after leaving the entrance to the Underworld, Odysseus sailed towards an island where strange creatures called Sirens lived. Half-woman and half-bird, they sang so sweetly that seafarers sailed in among the dangerous rocks surrounding the island to hear them better. Many ships were lost as the crews tried to follow the alluring voices, and many shipwrecked sailors had provided the Sirens with a good meal, for they lived on human flesh. Odysseus had been warned by Circe that neither he nor his men would be safe once they had heard the magic song. Yet Odysseus was very curious and wanted to hear the Sirens singing so he put wax in the ears of all his sailors but left his own ears unblocked. Then he told his sailors to tie him to the mast of the ship. So, with Odysseus tied to the mast and the sailors all as good as deaf, the ship sailed nearer the island. There was little wind and the sailors rowed hard and heard nothing of the singing. Only Odysseus heard it, and so lovely was the song that he struggled to break his bonds and swim ashore. But the ropes held fast and even though he shouted to his sailors to cut him loose, they could not hear him. Only when the Sirens' island disappeared over the horizon did they untie Odysseus and take the wax from their ears.

Soon they came to an even more dangerous place. Their ship had to pass between two terrible monsters. One, called Charybdis, was enormous and lived under the sea. When a ship come near, Charybdis sucked in water and made a terrible whirlpool which dragged everything on the surface down to the bottom of the sea. The only way a ship could avoid the whirlpool was by sailing close to a great rock. But in a cave on the rock lurked another monster called Scylla, who had six heads on long snake-like necks and twelve terrible paws. And every one of Scylla's six mouths would try to grab any sailor who came within reach.

When Odysseus' ship came to the whirlpool the sailors were so terrified that they dropped their oars. "Row, friends, row to the other side," cried Odysseus, "or we shall be sucked under!" The sailors took heart and pulled on the oars and their ship escaped the whirlpool. But they came too close to the rock where Scylla waited. Suddenly six heads with huge crocodile-like jaws grabbed six sailors and tore them from the ship. No man could fight Scylla and the other sailors could do nothing but row furiously to get away from the rock. So they escaped, but Odysseus had lost six of his companions.

Next they came to a pleasant green island. How glad they were to cast anchor and rest after their terrible adventures. But when Odysseus saw great herds of cattle as white as snow, he knew that these were the herds of the Sun God. Remembering Tiresias' warning, Odysseus told his sailors not to touch a single animal. He said that if they wanted to eat they should catch fish. But while Odysseus slept, his men said: "We have lived on fish long enough. It is time we had some real meat." Without another thought they killed some cows, cooked the meat and began to eat. When Odysseus awoke and saw what had happened, he was very angry with the sailors. He refused to take part in the meal and went hungry. But the sailors took no notice and went on eating. The Sun God, however, had seen what had happened and complained to Zeus. And the King of the Gods swore he would punish the sailors.

Having rested, Odysseus and his men sailed away. But before long, dark clouds covered the sky, thunder crashed and a gale swept over the sea. Then an enormous wave shattered the boat. Odysseus managed to seize hold of a plank but his comrades were not so lucky and they were all drowned. After many hours the storm died down and Odysseus floated helplessly on his plank until the waves washed him up on the shores of another island. Exhausted, he lay down under a bush and fell asleep.

Now Odysseus' one friend among the gods was Pallas Athene, the Goddess of Wisdom. That night the goddess appeared in a dream to the daughter of the king of the island. In the dream the goddess said: "Are you not a lazy girl. Your cupboard is full of unwashed clothing. If a prince came tomorrow to court you, neither you nor your maidens would have any clean, white clothes." The princess's name was Nausicaa, and when she woke, she called her servants together and they took all their robes and dresses to the river and washed them until they were sparkling white. They laid them out in the sun, and as they waited for them to dry they played with a ball. Princess Nausicaa threw the ball too far and when it fell with a splash into the river they all shouted: "Oh, our ball, it's lost!" Their shouts woke Odysseus. The hero saw that the sea had ripped his clothes to pieces so he broke a leafy branch from a tree to cover himself and stepped out from his hiding place.

When the girls saw a bedraggled man with his hair and beard full of seaweed and his body covered in little else but the branch of a tree, they ran away. But Nausicaa remained and Odysseus told her his story. She invited him to her father's palace where he bathed, dressed in white robes and was given delicious food and drink. Great kindness was shown to Odysseus by Nausicaa and her parents, the king and queen. But his troubles were not yet over.★

★ Kovacs omits certain episodes of the Odyssey. The first adventure before meeting the Cyclops, concerned the Island of the Lotos-Eaters, from which he had to rescue his men from a life of blissful forgetfulness. After the Isle of Aeolus, Odysseus' wanderings took him to the land of the Laestrygonians, a race of cannibals, before his arrival at Aeaea, the island of Circe. P.S.

11. Return to Ithaca

Odysseus greatly enjoyed his stay on the island where Nausicaa and her parents had received him so hospitably. But he longed to return to his wife Penelope and his son who would by now have become a young man. One day the kind king said: "One of my own ships shall take you to Ithaca, your home." And so Odysseus, at long last, reached the island he had left twenty years before. He was asleep when the ship reached Ithaca, so the sailors carried him ashore, left some gifts beside him, and sailed away.

When Odysseus woke, a mist hung over the island and he wondered if he had really come home. Then, through the mist, he saw a tall beautiful woman carrying a spear. When he saw her shield and helmet he realized that it was the goddess Pallas Athene. "Great Goddess," he called, "is this Ithaca?" Pallas Athene smiled and waved her spear. The mist vanished and Odysseus could see for himself that he had indeed reached home. He kissed the earth, happy that his journey was over. But then the goddess spoke and said: "I have come to warn you, Odysseus, that after the Trojan War ended and you did not return, many great and powerful men thought you had been drowned in a storm. And, as your wife Penelope is beautiful and Ithaca is a rich island, they came and wanted to marry her. But Penelope refused them all; she waited faithfully for you and still hopes you are alive."

Pallas Athene continued: "But these unwelcome suitors did not go away. They stayed on and to this day they live in your palace. They command your servants, they eat your food and poor Penelope can do nothing to make them go. There are more than a hundred of them, and if they knew you were here they would kill you. Only by cunning can you hope to deal with that insolent crowd. But I will help you. I will make you look like an old beggar so that no one will recognize you."

At her touch, his skin grew wrinkled, his hair and beard became white, and his clothes turned to rags. Then Pallas Athene said: "Many of your servants are now on the side of the insolent suitors, but there is an old swineherd who has remained faithful. Go and ask him for food and shelter, but do not tell him who you are. Only one person must know, your son Telemachus, but no one else, not even Penelope herself."

Odysseus obeyed the goddess. Disguised as an old beggar he went to the swineherd who kindly gave him food and allowed him to stay. Later, Telemachus came to visit the swineherd. Odysseus still acted like a beggar, but when his son left, he walked a little way with him and, by the power of Pallas Athene, Odysseus revealed his true self to his son. When Telemachus saw the tall, strong man he knew in his heart that this was really his father and he rejoiced. But Odysseus told him that no one must know of his return. So Telemachus returned to the palace, and Odysseus went back to the swineherd as a beggar.

The next day, Odysseus went with the swineherd to the palace. At the palace door an old dog called Argus was lying in the sun. Odysseus had often gone hunting with Argus in the days before he set out for Troy. Now that the dog was old, no one cared for the poor creature and it had to sleep outside and eat scraps it found in the street. When Odysseus came near, the old dog opened its eyes. Argus was too weak to sit up, but it wagged its tail. Seeing the dog brought tears to Odysseus' eyes, but he had to pretend he did not know the animal. Instead he patted Argus on the head lightly. The dog licked his hand, then the faithful old animal put its head on its forepaws and died.

Odysseus went into the palace. The suitors, more than a hundred of them, were having a great banquet. They ate choice dishes made from food grown on Odysseus' farms and drank fine red wine from his cellar. Calmly, the king disguised as a beggar went round the hall asking for a crust of bread to put into a little bag he carried. Some suitors gave him a morsel, others only cursed him and told him to go away, and some even kicked him. But Odysseus never showed the fury in his heart.

Penelope had stayed in her rooms. She hated the sight of the suitors enjoying her husband's food, wine and hospitality. When she heard that there was a strange beggar wandering round the banqueting hall she sent for him. And so Odysseus saw his wife again, but, of course, she did not recognize him. Then the queen asked if, as he wandered from place to place, he had ever heard news of her husband. And the beggar answered: "Yes, I have, I think he is on his way home and he cannot be very far away." Penelope was overjoyed and she told her servants to make the old beggar comfortable. That night, Pallas Athene appeared to Penelope in a dream and told her that she should arrange a contest among the suitors and promise to marry the man who won.

The next day the suitors were feasting again and the old beggar was going from table to table when Penelope entered the banqueting hall. She carried an enormous bow and a quiver of arrows. Telemachus followed and set up twelve axe heads so that the holes for the handles were all in a line. Then Penelope said: "My husband Odysseus used to be able to shoot an arrow from this bow through the twelve holes in the axe heads. If anyone here can accomplish such a feat, I shall marry him." Then she left the banqueting hall and went back to her rooms.

One by one the suitors took the bow that had belonged to Odysseus. Each pulled with all his strength, but not one of them could even bend the bow to put the bow-string on. Finally the old beggar said: "Let me see if there is still any strength left in my old bones?"

"Are you mad?" the suitors shouted. "A wretched beggar trying a king's bow?"

Then Telemachus spoke: "Only I can say who shall try my father's bow. Give it to the beggar!"

The beggar took the bow and casually bent it without effort to slip the bow-string on. He plucked the string lightly to test it, and it twanged with a high clear sound. The suitors grew pale when they heard it. Then he put an arrow on it, drew back the string and sent the arrow straight through all twelve holes. At that moment the disguise fell from him. Odysseus stood there, no longer a bent, wrinkled old man, but a wide- shouldered, tall king. The suitors were now his targets and his arrows never missed. One after another they fell. Some drew their swords but they were shot down before they reached Odysseus. Others tried to hide under tables or run away but Telemachus and the faithful swineherd stood armed with spears at the door. So Odysseus made them pay for Penelope's tears and suffering during the long years he was away.

Fearful and trembling Penelope had listened to the sound of the fighting. But when it was all over, she heard a firm tread which she knew and had waited for through so many years. And then her husband, Odysseus, came in, no longer an old beggar, no longer a warrior cutting down his enemies, but a man who had suffered great hardships. Now, at long last, Odysseus could live in peace and happiness with his faithful wife and dear son. *

---

* Another persistent tradition is that Odysseus did not stay in Ithaca, but took an oar over his shoulder and resolved not to stop wandering until he found a land where no-one knew the purpose of the oar. P.S.

The Argonauts

12. Jason, Heir to the Throne

The kingdom of Iolcos in Greece was ruled by King Aeson to whom a baby son called Jason was born. The child would one day become one of the great heroes of Greece, but when he was still a baby, Jason almost lost his life. It happened in this way: Jason's father, the king, had a younger brother, called Pelias. But Pelias was envious because he wanted to be king himself. Secretly he gathered together a band of armed men and one day he came with his army and attacked the palace of the rightful king. King Aeson was killed and Pelias would have killed Jason too but his mother escaped with him in her arms. She fled from the country and Pelias became king.

Jason's mother was afraid to go into cities or villages fearing that Pelias' men would find and kill her child and so the poor woman wandered through wild parts of the land where nobody lived. She was at the end of her strength, exhausted by hunger and thirst, when she was found by some strange creatures called Centaurs who were half-man and half-horse. They brought the mother and child to their king and leader, Chiron. Chiron was kind to them and, when the mother died soon afterwards, he looked after Jason and brought him up as if he was his own son.

Jason grew up to be a strong and handsome young man, and when he was twenty Chiron told him what had happened — how his uncle Pelias had wrongfully made himself king. Jason decided he would regain the kingdom that should, by rights, belong to him. The people of Iolcos did not like Pelias and hoped that the rightful heir would return. There was also a prophecy, which even the evil King Pelias got to hear, that one day a man wearing only one sandal would come from the wilderness and claim the throne.

So Jason set out from the land of the Centaurs. On his journey he came to a river swollen by heavy rain. On the bank stood an old woman who wanted to cross. Jason was a kind young man and he offered to carry her over. He helped her to get on to his broad shoulders and waded into the river. The old woman had seemed very frail and thin, and Jason thought she would be easy to carry. But once he got into the water she seemed to get much heavier. In the end she was so heavy that it took him all his strength to carry her. Under the heavy load his feet sank deep into the muddy riverbed; so deep that one of his sandals got stuck and he had to slip his foot out to carry on.

So with one foot bare he arrived on the other bank and put the old woman down. But when Jason looked at her again he saw that she was no longer a frail old woman; standing before him in all her majesty was Hera, the Queen of the Gods and the wife of Zeus. And Hera said: "As you have been helpful to an old woman in need, so shall I be helpful to you when you are in need."

Soon after, Jason arrived in the city where King Pelias ruled. When the people saw this tall young man coming from the wilderness, wearing only one sandal, they gathered around him and cheered. Jason walked straight into the palace and no one dared to stop him. At last he came before King Pelias, who, when he saw that the young man had only one sandal, grimly remembered the prophecy. Jason told him quite openly how he had been saved and brought up by the Centaurs. Then he said: "I have not come to encourage more bloodshed between us, l only want you to give me back what is mine by right: the crown and the rulership of the land. However, I am willing, as the rightful king, to give you a large piece of land where you can rule in peace."

Pelias did not like what he heard, but he did not dare to refuse such a fair proposal. Instead he thought of a way to get rid of Jason. He said: "I am quite willing to hand the crown over to you. But, you see, a few nights ago I had a dream. In the dream Zeus spoke and said. 'Only the man who can bring back the Golden Fleece is worthy to be king of the land of Iolcos.' When I woke I thought I would have to go and get the Golden Fleece. But as you are going to be the king it must be your task." Jason replied: "So be it, I shall go and bring back the Golden Fleece."

13. The Golden Fleece

Before we go on with Jason's adventures we shall hear the story of the Golden Fleece. A long, long time before Jason, there was a king in Iolcos whose wife had died. He had married another woman who became the stepmother of his two children, a boy called Phrixus and a girl called Helle. The stepmother hated the two children and made life miserable for them. The children would often sit together in the hills and comfort each other. They often thought of running away but Phrixus and Helle knew that they would not get far before they were caught and brought back. Then their stepmother would only make things worse for them.

Whenever they went walking in the hills, they asked the gods to help them escape. One day they felt more downhearted than ever and, as they prayed, bitter tears ran down their faces. Then suddenly they saw something moving on the hillside, something big that gleamed like gold. They ran to get a closer look and found an enormous sheep. The ram had mighty horns and its fleece was made of pure gold. The animal did not run away but stood quietly as if it was waiting for something. Then Phrixus said to his sister: "Look, he is big enough to carry both of us. Come on, let's get on his back."

They climbed on and rode the ram as if it was a pony. The animal did not seem to mind and walked on with Phrixus and Helle on its back. But when the golden ram reached the top of a hill, something quite unexpected happened. It rose up into the air and flew, carrying the children away from Iolcos and their evil stepmother. And Phrixus and Helle were really happy that they had escaped. After a time they flew over a narrow stretch of sea which separated two points of land which is called a strait. Above the strait a terrible wind blew. Phrixus cried: "Hold fast," but Helle was not strong enough and she fell into the sea and was drowned. Ever since, this strait has been called the Hellespont. Even today this narrow channel, which runs through Turkey and separates Europe from Asia, is called the Hellespont.

At long last the golden ram came down in the Kingdom of Colchis. The King of Colchis received Phrixus with great kindness and let the boy stay with him. Phrixus decided to sacrifice the ram to the gods who had sent the creature to the children as they prayed on the hillside. When the ram had been killed on the altar of the gods, Phrixus took the skin with all the golden wool on it and gave it to his friend the King of Colchis. The king was very pleased with the gift; no other king owned anything like it and he hung it in a tree in a garden called the Grove of Ares.

Ares, or Mars as the Romans called him, was the God of War and only men who had proved their courage were allowed to enter the grove. To make sure that no one tried to take the Golden Fleece, the Queen of Colchis, who had magic powers, called up a great dragon to guard it.

All this happened long before Jason was born. However, in time, the people of Iolcos, the land from which Phrixus had fled, learnt what had happened. The kings of Iolcos had always thought that, since Phrixus had been a prince in their kingdom, the Golden Fleece should really belong to them. But no one had ever been brave enough to claim it and fight the dragon that guarded it. Now King Pelias had told Jason to fetch it, and Jason, who was quite fearless, had agreed.

As soon as Jason announced that he was setting out for Colchis to get the fleece, many brave men volunteered to go with him. Jason was glad to have their company and slowly a huge crowd assembled, including Jason's cousins who wanted to help him regain the crown. Even the son of King Pelias decided to go because he wanted to share the fame that would come to anyone who took part in such a great adventure. Many heroes from all over Greece came to join Jason. Orpheus, a musician who could play the lyre so wonderfully that lions and tigers lay down to listen, and Heracles, the strongest of them all, also joined the throng.

A big ship called the *Argo* was built for the journey and the men who sailed on her were called Argonauts. (The word *naut* means sailor in Greek.) And so their strange journey began.

14. The Voyage of the *Argo*

The good ship *Argo* and the Argonauts who sailed in her met many strange adventures on their journey to Colchis, the land where the Golden Fleece was kept. One day, as the ship was sailing close to the shore, the Argonauts saw an old man sitting on a rock eating or, at least, trying to eat, his midday meal. But as soon as he took a piece of meat in his hand something swooped down from the sky, tore the morsel from his hands, and flew away. That something was not a bird but a Harpy which had the body of a big vulture and the head of a woman. Now, two sons of the Wind God, Boreas, were among the Argonauts. They had been born with wings on their shoulders, and they flew from the ship and drove the horrible Harpy away.

The old man was very grateful and told the Argonauts of a great danger their ship would soon meet and how to save themselves from it. He said: "Soon you will reach a narrow stretch of water between two enormous rocks, called the Symplegades. But these are not ordinary rocks for as soon as anything moves between them they crash together at lightning speed and whatever lies between them is crushed." When the Argonauts asked how they could get their ship through, the old man told them what they should do.

So they sailed on and the next day they saw the Symplegades rising from the sea like two mighty towers. Nearer and nearer they sailed, and when they were quite close, Jason released a dove. As the dove flew between the two rocks they crashed together with a crack like thunder, then started to move back slowly to their places again. Just at that moment the Argonauts pulled on the oars with all their might, and the *Argo* passed through before the Symplegades crashed back together again. But they only just got through, for the rudder at the stern of the ship was caught and smashed. But that did not matter, it was only a piece of wood and could easily be replaced. When the danger was past, Jason thought sadly about the poor dove that had saved them. But just then the bird came fluttering down on his shoulder; it had been too swift to be caught.

The Argonauts had many more adventures on their journey but at last they reached the land of Colchis where they beached the boat and hid it among trees and thick-growing bushes. Jason made his way straight to King Aetes, the ruler, and told him that he had come to claim the Golden Fleece. King Aetes smiled a cruel smile and said: "My dear young man, you are quite welcome to take the Golden Fleece if you can. But before the fleece is yours you have to pass two tests, if you don't mind. First of all I want you to plough a field. If that sounds easy, I must warn you that the plough has to be pulled by some rather special bulls. And when you have done that you must sow some rather special seeds. They are dragon's teeth which were given to me by Ares, the War God."

Jason agreed to perform the two tasks, and the king made him and his companions welcome and looked after them well. But the Argonauts knew that King Aetes had a wicked plan in mind. However it was different with the king's daughter, Medea. As soon as the princess saw Jason she fell in love with him and wondered how she could help. Now Medea had strange powers; she was the niece of the famous enchantress Circe who turned Odysseus' companions into pigs, and she had learned about magic from her aunt. One day when Medea was alone with Jason she gave him some ointment to rub on his body before he went to plough with King Aetes' bulls. She also told him what he should do once he had sown the dragon's teeth. Lastly, she handed him a violet flower to take with him when he went to get the Golden Fleece.

In return Jason promised that when he had the fleece and was ready to sail away, he would take Medea with him. She would be his wife and become the queen once he had regained his father's throne. For it was only with Medea's help that Jason could pass the tests which King Aetes was sure would destroy him.

15. Sowing the Dragon's Teeth

The day of the tests came and the King of Colchis invited Jason and all his companions to the field of the War God, Ares, where the ploughing was to take place. Then the king led four big white bulls out on to the field. They seemed very tame and King Aetes yoked them to the plough and ploughed a straight deep furrow from one end of the field to the other. Then he took the yoke off the bulls, let them free, and said to Jason: "Now it is your turn."

But as Jason approached the bulls they became wild and roared. They were not ordinary bulls, for fiery sparks flew from their nostrils setting the grass around them alight. But Jason had used Medea's ointment and neither sparks nor flames could harm him. With his strong arms he forced the bulls under the yoke and ploughed his furrows as straight and deep as the king's.

King Aetes was not pleased that Jason had passed the first test; he had hoped the bulls would gore him with their horns and that the fire would burn him up. Yet the young man still had to sow the dragon's teeth in the furrows he had just ploughed. So Jason took the teeth and began to sow them in the earth. Now ordinary seeds of wheat or barley take quite a time to grow but it is not so with dragon's teeth. Jason had barely finished putting the last tooth in the soil when they began sprouting. But it was a very strange sprouting for wherever a dragon's tooth had been sown a sharp spear head appeared from the ground. Then the soil began to heave like the sea, and from each tooth sprouted a fully-armed warrior. Before Jason knew what had happened row upon row of fierce-looking soldiers stood in the field. They all looked at him, raised their spears, and with a wild roar made ready to attack.

Just in time Jason remembered what Medea had told him to do. He picked up a stone and threw it at a warrior. It bounced off the warrior's shield and hit another one's helmet. The second soldier shouted at the first: "Why did you throw a stone at me," and lashed out at him with his sword. The next moment the two warriors were fighting each other. Then the ones next to them took sides and joined in. It was not long before all the warriors in the field were attacking each other with spear and sword and dagger. It was a terrible battle which only ended when they were all dead. And so Jason survived the second test. Of course the king was very disappointed. He had been certain that Jason would be killed by the warriors who had grown from the dragon's teeth, the gift of the War God.

But the king still hoped that Jason would be killed by the dragon which guarded the Golden Fleece. He told him how to get to the Grove of Ares and Jason set out immediately. But it was a long way and by the time Jason found it darkness had fallen. Yet there was a bright, full moon so he could see clearly in the silvery light. The garden was not at all a beautiful orchard for the foul breath of the dragon had withered all that once grew in it. The bare earth was covered with rocks, and the branches and trunks of the leafless trees were twisted into fantastic shapes.

But there was one bright spot in the garden. Gleaming in the moonlight, the Golden Fleece hung from the branches of an old oak tree. Below lay the dragon, resting at the foot of the tree, but when it saw Jason it stirred, ready to destroy the intruder.

Once again it was Medea's help that saved Jason. He held out the violet flower the princess had given him and the dragon sniffed its scent. Then the monster yawned, lay down and fell asleep. Jason took the Golden Fleece from the tree and hurried back to where the Argo was hidden. His companions were already waiting for him. Medea, who had escaped from her father's palace in the dark, was also waiting to join Jason and the Argonauts.

It was still night when the Argo sailed away with Medea and the Golden Fleece on board. By the time the King of Colchis woke the next morning, the ship was already far out at sea. The king was almost mad with fury; not only had he lost the Golden Fleece, but his daughter, Medea, had gone too. He sent ships to catch the Argonauts but it was too late — his daughter and the Golden Fleece were gone forever.

After many adventures the Argo arrived at Iolcos. But King Pelias was not willing to keep his promise and sent a large army to keep Jason out of the kingdom. The Argonauts could have easily fought and overcome the army, but one of them was Pelias' son and he did not want to fight against his father. And Jason still did not want to go to war against his uncle. Once again it was Medea who found a way out.

The Argonauts pretended to sail away, but first they put Medea ashore outside the city. She made herself look like a very old woman and went to the court of King Pelias. She told him she had magic powers that could make old people young again. Pelias, who was getting old, asked Medea for proof, so she changed herself back into a young and beautiful woman. The king was convinced and happy to drink the potion she gave him. It was, however, poison, and it killed him. Once the king was dead his soldiers no longer had the heart to fight. So Jason and the Argonauts returned and he and Medea were crowned King and Queen of Iolcos. And the Golden Fleece was hung up in the Temple of Ares.

Perseus

16. A Gift for the King

Seriphos is one of the many little islands in the sea which surrounds Greece. One day a fisherman casting his nets saw a great wooden chest floating in the sea. Wondering what treasure the chest contained, he threw a rope around it and pulled it ashore. To his great surprise he heard voices inside, and when he opened it he found a beautiful lady and a little boy. "Who are you? And how did you get yourself locked up in the chest?" asked the fisherman. The woman replied: "My name is Danae. I am the daughter of the King of Argos and this child is my son, Perseus. His father is Zeus himself. But wise priests told my father that his grandson would take his life and throne from him. So he gave orders to put us in a chest, and had us thrown into the sea, hoping we would both die. But Zeus has protected us and brought us safely here."

The fisherman took Danae and little Perseus to the king of the island. At first the king was kind to them and even asked Danae to become his wife. But when she refused the king became very angry. He said: "If you do not want to be the queen you will be a servant." And from then on the poor woman was an ill-treated servant at his court.

Perseus, meanwhile, grew up to become a handsome, strong young man. It hurt him very much to see his mother so badly treated and he wondered if he could do something to help. Perhaps, thought Perseus, I could give the king a wonderful present to make him behave more kindly to Danae.

One day there was a great festival and everybody brought presents for the king. Perseus came and said: "I have no possessions. My mother and I are poor, but perhaps I can do some service which will give you pleasure." With a crafty smile the king said: "Yes, there is something you could do which would please me very much. Far beyond the sea in a cave live three sisters called the Gorgons. They are monsters and two of them are immortal. The one who can be killed is called Medusa, but she is the worst of them all. Her face is so terrible that anyone who sees her is turned to stone. No living man knows what she looks like, for all who have seen her have been turned to stone. Now, if you could cut off Medusa's horrible head and bring it to me, I would be very pleased indeed."

Perseus set out without hesitation, for he would do anything if it would help his mother. But how he would get to the cave of the Gorgons and cut off the Medusa's head he did not know. But on his journey, Pallas Athene, the Goddess of Wisdom, and Hermes, the Messenger of the Gods, suddenly appeared before him. Pallas Athene said: "Your father, Zeus, has sent us to help you. Here, take my shield. It is made of metal so brightly polished that it is like a mirror. Now, when you come to the Gorgons' cave you must walk in backwards and hold the shield so you can see reflected in it what is behind you. Medusa's reflection cannot do any harm, but if you look at her face directly, you will be turned to stone. Medusa is easy to recognize for every hair on her head is a writhing, twisting serpent."

Then Hermes said: "I will give you this sword curved like a crescent moon. Use it to cut off the Medusa's head, but remember, watch her image in the shield; do not look at her. With the shield and sword you can kill and behead the monster. But you still need someone to show you how to get to the Gorgons' cave. So you must visit three sisters called the Grey Ones who are also monsters. They will tell you how to find the cave. They will also tell you what other things you need and how to get them."

17. The Gorgons' Cave

Perseus had received two gifts: Pallas Athene's shield to use as a mirror so that he would not have to look at Medusa's face, and a sword from Hermes that was curved like a new moon. But he still had to find the way to the Gorgons' cave and for this he needed the help of three monsters called the Grey Ones.

Pallas Athene and Hermes took him to the cave where the Grey Ones lived. Then Pallas Athene said: "These three sisters are not evil, but they are horrible looking creatures. You see, between them they have only one eye and one tooth, and they use them in turn. When one sister has finished using them, she gives them to the next and so they manage to get about, one at a time, while the other two wait their turn in the cave. But now Hermes and I can help you no more. You must find out how to make the Grey sisters tell you what you need to know." And the two gods disappeared. Quietly Perseus hid himself in the cave where two of the sisters were sleeping. The third one, who had the eye and the tooth, was away. It was not long before she returned and cried out: "Wake up, sisters. I am putting the eye and tooth on the table for the next one." But as soon as the third sister put the eye and tooth down Perseus sprang from his hiding place and snatched them. The monsters groped about on the table but there was nothing there, and they began to quarrel. Then Perseus called out: "Do not quarrel, beautiful ladies. I have your precious eye and tooth, but I will give them back if you tell me what I want to know." The Grey Ones cried out with dismay; they were quite helpless and they pleaded with him to return their precious possessions.

Then Perseus said: "I want to find the cave of the Gorgons and cut off Medusa's head. You must tell me what I need for the task." The Grey Ones mumbled and grumbled, but in the end they said: "If you give back the eye and the tooth, one of us will show you the way to a cave on the seashore. The mermaids, who are half-human and half-fish, live there. You must ask them for three things: a pair of shoes for your feet; a helmet for your head; and a satchel with a strap to hang by your side. " So Perseus gave back the eye and tooth and one of the sisters showed him the way to the mermaids' cave.

The cave was a wonderful sight. The sea reached right into it and the mermaids swam and played between the rocks. When he called out to them they all stopped playing and swam to the ledge where he stood. "Dear ladies of the sea," Perseus said, "I need your help. I want to go to the cave of the Gorgons and cut off Medusa's head. But I need a pair of shoes, a helmet and a satchel from you."

The mermaids laughed and said; "You are a handsome young man. You should stay and play with us instead of going to see the horrible Gorgons." But Perseus begged them to help him and, in the end, the mermaids replied: "We like you, handsome stranger, and we shall give you what you want. But the shoes you have asked for are not ordinary shoes; they have wings and whoever wears them can fly. The helmet you ask for is also no ordinary helmet, for when you wear it no one can see you; you are invisible. And you need the satchel to put Medusa's head into once you have cut it off. Otherwise, if you carried it in your hand, anyone who looked at it, including yourself, would be turned to stone."

The mermaids brought Perseus the three things they had promised: the winged shoes; the helmet that made one invisible; and the satchel. He thanked them and put the shoes on his feet, the helmet on his head and hung the satchel by the strap from his shoulders. Then he quickly rose into the air and flew invisibly far across the ocean to a grim dark cave on the island where the Gorgons lived.

When Perseus came to the Gorgons' cave, he remembered Pallas Athene's advice and entered the cave backwards. With his left hand he held up the shield to see what was behind him. In his right hand he carried the curved sword of Hermes.

But he had only taken a few steps when he saw the mirror-image of the Gorgons. They were fast asleep, but even asleep they were horrible to look at. Their enormous bodies were covered in dragon scales and their teeth were like the tusks of a boar. Their hands were claws of iron, and they all had huge wings. The one called Medusa had hundreds of twisting, writhing snakes for hair. Even brave Perseus trembled when he saw the three monsters reflected in his shield. But he soon took heart. He stepped closer and, looking carefully into the mirror of the shield, beheaded Medusa with one stroke. The snakes hissed and twisted for a moment, then lay still. Perseus put the sword in its scabbard and, reaching behind, picked up the head by the snake hair. The satchel opened by itself and he quickly put the head inside.

Then something very strange happened. From Medusa's neck sprang a beautiful white winged horse called Pegasus, and a golden giant called Chrysaor. But Perseus did not stay to marvel at these things. Already the other two Gorgons had begun to stir, so he hurried from the cave and, carried by his winged shoes, rose into the air. But the other two Gorgons had found their dead sister. They came out of the cave roaring, unfolded their great wings and flew into the air, searching for the culprit. But the helmet made Perseus invisible so the Gorgons could not see him and he escaped. Soon the grim island of the Gorgons was far away and Perseus flew, as light as a cloud, over oceans and foreign lands towards his home.

Now, one of the countries he flew over was Ethiopia. The King and Queen of Ethiopia had a very beautiful daughter called Andromeda. The queen was so proud of her daughter's beauty that she boasted that not even the fair daughters of the Sea God, the mermaids, were as lovely as her own Andromeda. The Sea God was, however, just as proud of his daughters, and he was so angry about the queen's boasting that he sent a sea dragon up out of the waves. By day it devoured humans and animals and at night it went back into the sea.

The King of Ethiopia was in despair and he went to a temple where there was a wise priestess who could understand the will of the gods. These temples were known as oracles and there were many of them in the ancient world. Whenever people had problems and did not know what to do, they went to an oracle and asked the priest or priestess for advice. And the priestess told the King of Ethiopia: "Only when your daughter, Andromeda, is sacrificed to the dragon will the Sea God forgive you."

The king was horrified. How could he allow his own beloved, beautiful daughter to be devoured by the dragon? But when the people of Ethiopia heard the oracle's advice they cried: "We love our sons and daughters as much as you love your child. It is better that one girl should die so the rest of us can live in peace."

For the sake of his people the king had to agree that his daughter, Andromeda, be given to the dragon. So the beautiful princess was taken to the seashore and bound to a rock where the dragon would find her next time it came up from the ocean.

18. Perseus to the Rescue

Once Perseus had escaped from the Gorgons he no longer needed to wear the helmet which made him invisible so he had tied it to the satchel which held Medusa's head. Then, as he flew over Ethiopia, he saw a girl tied to a rock on the seashore far below. Poor Andromeda had been left alone, bound to the rock, for no one wanted to be near her when the dragon came up from the sea. Terrified, she had given up all hope, so Andromeda was astonished when she looked up and saw a young man descending from the air. As soon as Perseus reached the ground he asked: "Fair lady, why are you bound to the rock?"

As Andromeda told him her story it seemed to Perseus that he had never seen a more beautiful maiden. But she had hardly finished her tale when the sea began to churn as if it were boiling and, out of the depths, the monster appeared. Perseus leapt into the air as the beast's huge jaws snapped at him. Swooping from the air like an eagle, he landed on the dragon's back and plunged Hermes' sword into the monster's body. Then he flew away as the wounded monster sank down into the ocean depths.

After Perseus untied Andromeda and took her back to her parents there was great rejoicing all through Ethiopia. He asked if he could marry Andromeda and the king said yes, so a wedding feast was prepared.

But there was one man who did not share the happy mood at the royal court and that was the king's brother, Phineus. Before the dragon had come from the sea, Andromeda, his niece, had been promised to him as a bride. Although Phineus had not gone to help her when she was tied to the rock, he was angry that she now planned to marry another man. Phineus felt that he had been cheated and thought of a way to prevent the marriage.

On the day of the wedding, while the guests were still eating, drinking and toasting the young couple, two hundred armed warriors suddenly stormed in. Led by Phineus, they struck down any guest who got in their way as they tried to attack Perseus. At first Perseus defended himself with the good sword of Hermes, but he soon saw that there were too many enemies and he could not hope to escape. Then he realized that courage alone was not enough and he called out: "All those who are my friends, close your eyes! Do not look at me!" Closing his own eyes tightly, Perseus plunged his hand into the satchel he always wore slung across his shoulder and drew out the Medusa's head. He held it up, and Phineus and all his men turned to stone. Then Perseus put the head back into the satchel and told the wedding guests to open their eyes.

Having gained the beautiful Andromeda, Perseus was anxious to return to his mother. But now that he had a wife he could not use his winged boots so the couple travelled by sea. At last they came to Seriphos, the island where Danae, Perseus' mother, was living as an ill-treated servant. Perseus and his bride found Danae in the Temple of Zeus. Crying with joy, his mother embraced him and explained that she had fled to the temple because it was the only place where she was safe from the evil king.

19. A Fateful Throw of the Discus

Perseus told his wife, Andromeda, and his mother, Danae, to wait in the Temple of Zeus until he came back. Then he set off to see the King of Seriphos, who had not only treated his mother so cruelly but had also sent Perseus to the Gorgons' cave in the hope that he would never return. The king was greatly surprised when Perseus arrived. He sneered at him and said: "Well, so the hero has come back, but I don't see the Medusa's head. Perhaps you will find enough courage to cut off chickens' heads when I put you to work as a kitchen boy." But Perseus answered: "I have done what you asked of me. And now you shall see for yourself." He closed his eyes and when he took the Medusa's head from the satchel, the king immediately turned to stone.

Then Perseus put the head back into the satchel and left the palace. He had not gone far when two shining figures appeared which he recognized as Pallas Athene and Hermes. He knelt down before the two gods and said: "With your help I have accomplished the task I set out to do, and now I can gratefully return the things you lent me. To you, Pallas Athene, I give back the shining shield which helped me in Gorgons' cave. The head of Medusa shall also be yours, for its terrible power should not be entrusted to human beings. And to you Hermes, I return the curved sword. The winged shoes, the helmet that made me invisible, and the satchel I also give to you so that they may be returned to the mermaids who were also very kind to me."

So Perseus gave the gods back all the things which they had lent him for the great adventure. Later on, Pallas Athene put the head of the Medusa on her shield and only the enemies of wisdom had to fear the face that turns living men into stone.

But the adventures of Perseus had not ended yet. He did not

wish to live on the island where his mother had suffered. So he found the fisherman who, many years before, had rescued the chest in which he and his mother had been thrown into the sea. Perseus made him King of Seriphos. Then Andromeda, Danae and Perseus sailed away to Argos, the land of his grandfather. Now you remember that it was Perseus' grandfather who had ordered that they be thrown into the sea because of a prophecy. But Perseus did not have any wish for revenge. By now the grandfather, if he was still alive, would be an old man and Perseus was willing to forgive him for what he had done.

On the journey back to Argos they stopped at a port called Larissa. There were garlands of flowers everywhere and they saw many people dressed up as if for a feast. When Perseus asked what they were celebrating, the people answered: "This is the day of our great games. Many young men from all over Greece have come to take part." And when Perseus heard that there would be racing, wrestling and spear and discus-throwing competitions, he decided to stay and throw the discus.

Now the Greeks were the very first people to hold such games. The contests took place inside a stadium, which was a large field surrounded by tiers of stone benches for the spectators. The spectators were not only from Larissa itself; many visitors from all over Greece had flocked to watch. After the wrestling, racing and spear throwing, the discus throwing began. Every man who took part was allowed three throws and Perseus was the last to try his luck.

The crowd cheered after Perseus' first throw, for the discus spun through the air and went further than any man had thrown it before. When he threw again, the discus flew from one end of the field to the other. The spectators stood up and shouted with excitement; this was a feat that no one had ever achieved before. Now Perseus made his third throw and the discus flew up in a high and wide arc. But at that moment a strong gust of wind caught it and carried it away from the field. The discus came hurtling down where the spectators were sitting and hit an old man on the head. As he fell from his seat there was a hush all over the stadium. Perseus rushed to the seat where the man had fallen, but when he reached the man he was already dead.

Perseus asked who the man was and a spectator told him: "He is the King of Argos." It was Perseus' grandfather, Danae's father, who had put his daughter and her child in a chest to be thrown into the sea.

So the prophecy had come true — Perseus had, without meaning to, killed his grandfather. He was, of course, very upset and he went to the Temple of Zeus to ask forgiveness. There the priests told him that it was not his fault: it had been ordained by fate that the King of Argos should die in this way.

Perseus, Andromeda and Danae continued their journey to Argos where Perseus became the new king and ruled for many years in peace and happiness. But the story of his adventures was remembered in Greece for a long time. The Greeks named a group of stars in the sky after him. Another group is called Andromeda and, nearby, there is also a group called Draco, which means dragon or monster. So the story of Perseus, Andromeda and the Sea God's dragon is written in the sky.

The Twelve Labours
of Heracles

20. The Milk of a Goddess

Perseus and Andromeda became King and Queen of Argos. After they died, their children and then their children's children ruled the kingdom of Argos. Then it happened that Alkmene, the great-granddaughter of Perseus, gave birth to a son. But the child's father was not a human being; it was Zeus, the King of the Gods. Hera, Zeus' wife, was very angry that a mortal woman should have a child fathered by a god. The thought that Zeus should have cared more for a mortal woman than for herself, a goddess and his wife, made her furious.

Even after Zeus left Alkmene and she married King Amphitryon, who became the child's foster-father, Hera still hated both mother and son. But Zeus wanted Alkmene's child to become a hero stronger and greater than any other.

One night he sent Hermes, the Messenger of the Gods, down to earth to the palace of King Amphitryon and Queen Alkmene. Hermes carried the child up to Mount Olympus. And while Hera was fast asleep, the little child was put to her breast to drink the milk of the goddess. By drinking this milk, the child received strength such as no human being had ever possessed. But drinking the milk of an immortal goddess also meant that he would not go down into the Underworld when he died, but join the gods in the heights of Olympus. Then Hermes took the child back to its cradle in the palace. And that child, who had drunk the milk of the gods, was called Heracles by the Greeks and Hercules by the Romans.

Hera, however, got to know what had happened that night and she was furious. She was so angry that she decided to destroy the child. One night when little Heracles was asleep in his cradle in his mother's room, two black snakes, sent by Hera, slithered over to the cradle and glided into the child's bed. At that moment Heracles woke up and, when he saw the two snakes' heads hovering above him, he stretched out his little hands, caught them by their necks and strangled them.

Just then Alkmene woke up. She saw the snakes in her child's cradle and screamed. King Amphitryon, who was very fond of his stepson, heard his wife's cry and came rushing in with a sword in his hand. But to their surprise little Heracles was unharmed and the two snakes were dead. Soon after, King Amphitryon called a wise priest and asked what the future held for Heracles. The priest answered: "He will slay many monsters. He will go through hardships such as no other man has ever suffered, but when his days on earth are over he will join the gods high on Olympus."

As Heracles grew up, famous men became his teachers. They taught him to use the bow and arrow so that he never missed his mark, to drive chariots and to throw the javelin. He also learned to recite poetry and play the lyre. Most of all he loved the songs telling how his ancestor, Perseus, had overcome Medusa and the dragon.

But his terrible strength, which had come to him through the goddess Hera's milk, also brought him unhappiness. Now, of all his teachers he liked best the wise Linos, an old man who taught him to play the lyre. But young Heracles, who could out-do everyone else in feats of strength, was not very good with his fingers when it came to plucking the lyre strings. He often played a wrong note and every time this happened Linos said: "Wrong again, you must be more careful!" One day Heracles was so angry that his music did not improve that he threw the lyre away. It flew through the air with enormous force and hit his teacher on the head, killing the old man instantly.

Heracles wept bitter tears of remorse; he had killed the teacher he loved. It was not murder for he had not meant to kill Linos, but, as a punishment for his bad temper, he had to leave the palace and live as a shepherd in the hills of Argos.

21. The Path of Virtue

After Heracles went to live with the shepherds in the hills of Argos, he was often alone with his sheep. On these occasions he used to wonder what his future might be. Would he become the king and rule Argos, would he enjoy riches and power, or should he seek adventure? One day, as he was deep in thought, two women appeared to him. One was beautiful, but her whole bearing was modest and she wore only a simple white robe. The other woman was pretty too, but in a different way. She wore make-up, her nails were painted, and her dress was red, pink and orange.

The woman in the colourful dress seemed very pleased with herself. She preened like a peacock, and every movement she made was calculated to draw attention to herself. She turned and spoke to Heracles: "My dear young man," she said, "I see you are undecided about your future. Now, if you choose me for a friend, I shall guide you on a path of ease and comfort. You will not encounter any hardship, nor will you have to do any hard work. Instead you will enjoy exquisite food and drink, and be free to go from one amusement to the next. If there is anything unpleasant like hard work to be done, you need not worry; I will see to it that others will always do it for you."

"Who are you?" asked Heracles.

"People call me Pleasure," said the woman. "And I am liked by everyone, for, as you can see, I am very beautiful, don't you think?"

Heracles did not answer. He turned to the other woman and asked her: "And who are you?"

The modest woman in the white dress answered: "People call me Virtue, which means strength to do what is right, even if it is unpleasant, hard or dangerous. If you follow my path in life, the path of virtue, you will have to face perils and pain. As soon as one task is finished, another will be waiting for you. There will be little reward, for what you do will benefit others, not yourself. But the whole of Greece will be grateful to you. Your deeds will be remembered in times to come and, whenever human beings face a hard task, they will think of you and tackle it with courage and confidence."

Quickly, Pleasure interrupted her, and said: "You can see for yourself, dear Heracles, that she has nothing to offer you. Just think of all the nice things I can give you; luxury, amusements, wealth. And you may have them all without any work at all."

For a moment Heracles looked at the two women, and then he made up his mind. "If I follow you, Pleasure, the strength which the gods have given me would be wasted," he said. "But even if I were weak, I would still choose Virtue. Whatever happens, I will follow the path of Virtue."

Now the question of whether we want to live only for our own pleasure and satisfaction, or whether we want to help others, comes to everyone sooner or later. Each one of us must decide whether to follow the path of pleasure or the path of virtue. Yet all the great accomplishments in the world were the work of men and women who decided to follow the hard path of virtue.

Shortly after Heracles made the decision to follow the path of virtue, he found an opportunity to do a good deed. At that time many parts of Greece were covered with forests inhabited by lions, boars, snakes and other wild animals. One of the lions had come out of the forest and was roaming the hills of Argos killing sheep. It had also killed several shepherds and when Heracles heard about this he set out, armed with a big club. He roamed the wild, wooded mountains until he found the lion.

As soon as the beast saw him it pounced, leaping high in the air. But Heracles quickly stepped aside. As the lion came down, he struck it such a heavy blow with his club that the beast's neck was broken. Heracles skinned it and, from then on, wore the lion skin over his shoulder. Sometimes he even wore the lion's head, with its huge gaping jaws, like a helmet.

22. The Oracle's Advice

But Heracles did not only fight against wild beasts. A foreign king, called Erginos, invaded Argos with a great army. Heracles and a small band of brave men attacked the invaders. When Erginos and his army saw that Heracles could kill an enemy with a single blow of his big fist, they were terrified and fled. King Erginos was only too pleased to make peace, and to show he was sincere he offered his daughter Megara as Heracles' wife.

So Heracles married Megara and was happy with his wife and the children she bore him. But the goddess Hera had not forgotten her old hatred of the hero; she would not let Heracles live in peace. One day he was making a sacrifice to the gods. His children were with him and they watched as he made a fire on the altar. As Heracles took his knife to sacrifice a sheep, Hera cursed him with madness. He could no longer think; he did not know what he was doing. In his confusion his children appeared to be enemies and he stabbed and killed them. Heracles fell unconscious to the ground, and when he woke the madness had left him. But his heart nearly broke with anguish when he saw what had happened. Without a word, Heracles left his house to become a homeless wanderer.

The first place Heracles came to was the most famous of all the oracles in Greece — the Temple of Apollo in the city of Delphi. The temple was built over a deep fissure through which smoke rose from the depths of the earth. Close to the crack stood a special three-legged chair, called a tripod, where the priestess sat as the smoke swirled about. People from all over Greece, and even from other lands, came to seek advice from the priestess at Delphi. Stimulated by the smoke, the priestess could contact the gods who would give answers to questions people asked.

Heracles went to the oracle and asked the priestess what he could do to make amends for killing his children. And the priestess answered: "Go to King Eurystheus of Mycenae and offer yourself as his servant. Twelve tasks he will give you. When you have accomplished these twelve deeds, you will have done so much good that you will be forgiven for killing your children and will no longer feel guilty."

So Heracles went to Mycenae. But when King Eurystheus saw the tall, strong young man, he was more afraid than pleased. He wanted was to get rid of Heracles and his terrible strength as soon as possible. So he said the first thing that came into his head: "Go and get me the skin of the lion that lives in the Nemean Fields." But the lion of the Nemean Fields was no ordinary lion, as Heracles soon found out.

When Heracles came to the Nemean Fields he discovered that all the peasants' houses were empty. Everybody had fled to escape from the lion. Armed with a bow, Heracles hid in some bushes and waited. After a while he saw the beast coming; it was an enormous creature with skin the colour of burning fire. Heracles took careful aim, but the arrow which flew from his bow barely made a scratch on the beast's tough skin. The lion did not even notice that it had been attacked. It just yawned and walked off towards the forest. Heracles followed and saw it go into a cave. Then he realized that if the bow was no help, a sword would not be much use either. He would have to tackle the lion with his bare hands, but the hero was not afraid.

When the lion saw Heracles coming, its mane bristled, a roar rumbled in its throat and, with one great leap, the beast pounced. But Heracles was ready for the attack. He grabbed the beast, clamped his arms around its neck and squeezed with all his iron strength until he had choked it to death. When he tried to skin the lion he found that his knife could not pierce the animal's tough skin. Eventually he discovered that the only way to cut the skin was to use the lion's own claws.

When Heracles returned to Eurystheus with the enormous lion's skin, the king nearly fainted. "I don't want to see these monsters you kill," he cried. "Next time you have completed your task, stay outside the city walls. You can send a messenger to let me know you are ready for the next deed. I don't want to see you or the game you have hunted. And now your next task is to kill the Hydra."

23. Hydra Beheaded

The killing of the Nemean lion was the first of the twelve tasks or twelve labours of Heracles. Twelve is a very important number. The Babylonians divided the day and the night into twelve hours each. There are also twelve months in the year, and Christ had twelve disciples when he was on earth.

The second of the twelve labours was to kill the Hydra, a giant snake with nine heads. But one of the Hydra's heads, the one in the middle, was immortal and could not be killed. Heracles took a chariot and asked his nephew Iolaos to be his charioteer. Iolaos drove the horses until they came to a great swamp where the monster lurked waiting for victims. When they caught sight of the Hydra, Heracles told Iolaos to wait while he went off to fight the beast.

The Hydra tried to escape and crawled into a cave, but Heracles lit a fire and shot burning arrows into the darkness. The fiery arrows soon brought the monster out. Enraged, it came for the hero with all nine heads hissing and nine forked tongues darting from its nine mouths. Heracles steadied himself and, with one blow of his club, crushed three of the evil-looking heads. But to his amazement, new heads sprouted from the necks; for every head he had crushed, two new ones appeared.

Heracles called Iolaos and asked him to come and help. He told his charioteer to set fire to a nearby wood and bring back burning logs. Then Heracles cut the Hydra's new heads off with his sword. As soon as a head was severed, Iolaos seared the stump with a red-hot log and no more heads grew from it. One after another the Hydra's heads came off until there was only one head left: the head that was immortal. That head could not be killed but it could be cut off and, with a swift stroke of his sword, Heracles severed the head from the neck. Then he rolled a heavy rock over it, so that it was buried and could do no more harm. After the fight was over Heracles dipped his arrows into the Hydra's black, poisonous blood. From now on even the slightest wound from one of his arrows would bring death.

When Eurystheus received the message that Heracles had accomplished the second labour he said: "He has shown he can kill by using his strength. Now let us see if he can also run fast. I want him to bring me the hind of the goddess Artemis." Artemis, or Diana, was the Goddess of Hunting and the hind Heracles had to catch was sacred to her. But it was not an ordinary female deer. The beautiful creature had golden antlers and hooves of brass and could run faster than any other animal.

Heracles' task was to capture the fleet-footed animal and, after a long search, he caught sight of the hind in a forest. But the hind ran away with great speed. Through forests and fields, uphill and downhill, Heracles chased the animal. He could not catch it, but he was always close enough to keep the animal in sight. And so the hunt went on and on, day and night, until, in the end, the hind had no strength left.

Exhausted and trembling with fear, the creature with golden antlers and hooves of brass sank to the ground. Just as Heracles gently lifted the hind on to his shoulders, the goddess Artemis appeared before him. "How dare you hunt the animal sacred to me," she said angrily. Heracles answered: "It is not my will, O goddess, to capture your hind. I do it as a servant of Eurystheus, whom I must obey by the will of the gods." So Artemis forgave him and let him go.

The exhausted hind was asleep when Heracles carried it to Eurystheus. But the king was too afraid to keep the hind for fear of making Artemis angry. At his command Heracles put the sleeping hind down in a nearby forest and, when the animal woke it leapt up and galloped away joyfully.

24. The Augean Stables

Heracles had accomplished his third task, the capture of the hind with the golden antlers. But Eurystheus said: "That task was really far too easy. The next labour, which is to capture the great wild boar that is also sacred to Artemis, will be much harder!"

On the way to the mountain where the wild boar lived, Heracles came to a mighty river. On the river banks lived some Centaurs, half-human and half-horse. One of the Centaurs, Pholon, invited Heracles to stay the night in the cave where he lived. Pholon prepared a hearty meal for his guest and even produced a special wine which he had kept for the day when Heracles would come.

The wine had a strong sweet smell and the other Centaurs, who were very fond of wine, sniffed and said: "There is something special going on and we want to share in it." They all crowded round the entrance to the cave but Heracles and Pholon told them to go away and to leave them in peace. This made the other Centaurs very angry and they picked up boulders and tree trunks and threw them at Heracles. This, in turn, roused Heracles' fury and he took up his bow and shot one of the Centaurs.

The others were very frightened and galloped away to find their king, Chiron, who was a wise Centaur. But Heracles, who was in one of his wild tempers, chased them and when he saw them crowding round Chiron, he fired another arrow which hit the wise Centaur. Now Chiron was immortal so he could not die, but the poison on the arrow spread through his body causing terrible pain. When Heracles saw Chiron suffering he was very sorry indeed. He tried all kinds of herbs to soothe the wounded Centaur but nothing would help. Deep in sorrow, Heracles said farewell to Chiron and left to hunt the wild boar. (Later he was able to end the Centaur's suffering.)

Heracles found the enormous boar deep in the forest and, with ringing shouts, drove it out from the thick undergrowth. The boar ran up into the mountains with Heracles close behind. Whenever the boar tried to turn downhill, Heracles headed it off. The beast's only possibility of escape was uphill and it ran higher and higher. Soon they reached the snow-covered heights where the boar got stuck in a snowdrift and could go neither backwards or forwards.

Heracles tied up the wild grunting boar with rope, put him on his shoulders and carried him down the mountain. But when he came to Mycenae, King Eurystheus' city, he took no notice of the king's orders and walked straight into the palace. When Eurystheus saw the enormous grunting beast, its eyes red with fury, he was so frightened that he ran from the hall down to the cellar and hid in a wine barrel. Heracles, having enjoyed his joke, took the boar to a temple and left it with the priests.

King Eurystheus was furious. The story of how he had hidden in a barrel became known and everybody laughed at him. In revenge, Eurystheus gave Heracles a task that was unworthy of a hero: to clean the stables of King Augeas in one day. Now, King Augeas had a great number of cows. He kept three thousand, including twelve of the Sun God's white oxen, in one big cow-shed. However, he was a very mean man, and the herdsmen who looked after the cattle were paid so badly that they could not be bothered to keep the cow-shed clean. In time the piles of dung in the stable grew so high that the cows stood in it up to their necks, and the smell was unbearable for miles around.

When Heracles went to Augeas and offered to clean out his stable, the king was so pleased that he promised one tenth of his herd as a reward. He expected the hero to take a shovel and start digging but Heracles did nothing of the sort. Instead he set to and made a big hole in one wall of the stable. He made another hole in the opposite wall, then dug a canal from a nearby river back to the cow-shed. Then Heracles blocked the riverbed with a dam so that the water rushed along the canal. It flowed into the stables through one hole in the wall and out the other before returning to its course. And in a few hours, the river had carried away the great piles of dung.

But King Augeas did not give Heracles the reward he had promised. Heracles was cheated but there was nothing he could do. The gods had ordered him to obey Eurystheus and he had to clean out the stables whether he was rewarded or not.

25. Taming the Twelve Mares

When Heracles got back to Mycenae, Eurystheus told him his next task was to drive away the Stymphalian Birds. The birds were enormous vulture-like creatures, with beaks and claws harder than iron. But even worse was the fact that they could fire their sharp, hard feathers into the air like arrows. Their feather-arrows could even pierce shields and armour, and countless men had been killed and devoured by the birds.

When Heracles came to the lake where the birds nested, he saw them flying in flocks so large that they darkened the sky like clouds. Many others sat on their nests on the ground. He felt helpless and wondered how he could drive them all away. Suddenly someone tapped him on the shoulder and when he turned round he saw Pallas Athene. The goddess smiled and said: "You need never despair for the gods will always help a man who tackles a task with courage." She gave him two enormous iron rattles which the god Vulcan had made. (Vulcan was the Blacksmith of the Gods and whenever a volcano erupted in flames, the Greeks and Romans said: "That's fire from the smithy of Vulcan.")

After Pallas Athene had gone, Heracles shook the rattles with all his might. They made such a horrible, deafening noise that the birds all rose into the air. They flew higher and higher then disappeared from view, and to this day nobody knows where they have gone.

Heracles' next task was much harder. He had to bring Eurystheus twelve mares that belonged to King Diomedes. The mares were so strong and savage that they had to be shackled in their stables with iron chains. And they did not feed on oats: any strangers who had the bad luck to come to the city where Diomedes ruled were thrown to the horses as food.

Heracles gathered some companions and they travelled by ship to the land of King Diomedes. When they arrived he told his friends to wait and went alone to the stables. He broke the horses' chains as if they were straw and took the beasts outside. With his terrific strength, Heracles tamed them all and led them back to the ship. But, by now, King Diomedes had discovered that his horses had been stolen so he gathered his warriors and set off in pursuit. Heracles and his men were waiting and a wild fight began. When the horses heard the sounds of battle they became savage again. They turned on the poor youngster who was looking after them and tore him to pieces before galloping into the battle. But it was King Diomedes they attacked. Their hooves shattered his helmet and shield. Then they bit him to death and drank his blood. After this the twelve mares became as tame as ponies and even a child could have ridden any one of them without harm.

Heracles sailed back to Mycenae. He took the horses to King Eurystheus who gave them to the priests of the Temple of Hera. The descendants of those horses became the mounts of great kings and heroes. And one day Alexander the Great had a horse, Bucephalus, which came from that breed.

26. Fearless Amazons

As the next task, King Eurystheus told Heracles he must capture the white bull belonging to King Minos who ruled the island of Crete. Even today, on that island, you can still see the remains of King Minos' splendid palace at a place called Knossos. Painted on the walls are scenes of life in those times, including some showing supple young men and women vaulting over great bulls.

Now King Minos had one special bull, a great white beast, that was said to have come from the sea. One day, the king promised that if his fleet came back safely to Crete he would sacrifice his famous white bull to the Sea God, Poseidon. Although the fleet returned, King Minos did not keep his word. He did not sacrifice the bull and Poseidon became so angry that he cursed the bull with madness. The huge beast ran wild, trampling crops and goring men. The whole island lived in terror but no one was brave enough to fight the bull, or to catch and tame it.

When Heracles arrived in Crete and offered to tame the raging beast, King Minos and all his people were only too pleased. Heracles went out and found the bull in a field. The bull lowered its head and roared. Its huge hooves tore up clumps of earth as the beast made ready to charge. But Heracles seized the bull by the horns, and with his mighty strength he forced the animal's head down towards the earth. The beast sank to its knees, recognizing that it had found its master. Now that the bull was tame, Heracles jumped on its back and, holding on by the horns, rode it to the seashore and right into the water.

Seated on the animal's back, Heracles made it swim across the sea to Mycenae and the court of King Eurystheus. The king was greatly surprised when he saw, from the tower of his palace, Heracles astride the bull. The priests of the Temple of Hera would not take the animal so Heracles set it free. Later the bull ran wild again and did much damage until another hero, called Theseus, killed it.

Heracles next task was to bring King Eurystheus the precious girdle of the Queen of the Amazons. The Amazons were strong women and fearless fighters. They were armed like warriors and hunted and fought wars just like men. But in their kingdom the only use they had for men was as slaves.

Heracles did not set out alone for this task for many heroes were proud to join him. When they came to the land of the Amazons, they were received very hospitably. The Queen of the Amazons was even quite willing to give her girdle to Heracles. But the goddess Hera was not pleased that Heracles should accomplish his task so easily. She changed into an Amazon herself and went among the women spreading the rumour that Heracles and his friends had come to take away their queen. Instantly the Amazons mounted their horses and attacked Heracles' camp. It was a furious battle and only Heracles' great strength saved the Greek warriors who had come with him.

Even the fiercest of the Amazons, the sister of the queen, was beaten by Heracles and taken as a prisoner to his ship. The other Amazons all fled but the queen came and pleaded for her sister to be set free. Heracles struck a bargain: he would let the sister go in exchange for the queen's girdle. And so he brought the girdle back to Eurystheus.

27. The Oxen of the Sun God

"There are only three more tasks left," Eurystheus said, "but I must make them much harder than the others were. From now on you must test your strength against powers which are not of this earth. Go now and bring me the oxen of the Sun God, Helios."

Now, the island where the Sun God's oxen grazed was far out in the ocean. Once Odysseus and his sailors had landed there. But after his men had killed and eaten one of the sacred cows, they lost their lives in a great storm. Since then no one had found the island. Even Odysseus himself would not have known how to find the way back across the trackless sea.

Heracles set out and sailed from island to island. He wandered through many lands but he found nobody who could tell him where the island lay. At long last he came to the end of all land and before him stretched an ocean that seemed endless. To mark the place where he could not go any further Heracles put up two great pillars. The Pillars of Heracles, as they were known, stood for many hundreds of years and no Greek sailor dared to go beyond them. The place where they once stood is known today as the Straits of Gibraltar.

As the sun beat down on the glittering ocean, Heracles cried out in despair: "Even you, the sun, have turned against me!" And he lifted his bow to shoot an arrow at the sun. At that moment Helios, the Sun God, appeared and said: "You are mistaken, Heracles. Every brave man, every hero is a friend of the sun and I want to help you." After Heracles explained how King Eurystheus had commanded him to capture the cattle, the Sun God said: "I will give you my own boat. All by itself the boat will carry you to and from the island. There, a monster dog and a terrible giant guard my cattle and you must overcome them. But you have nothing to fear from me."

The Sun God's great golden boat took Heracles across the

ocean to the island very quickly. Heracles saw the cattle grazing on green fields and went ashore. But a dog as big as an ox and a giant with three bodies, three heads, six arms and six feet, stood guarding the herd. Growling and snarling, the dog flew at Heracles' throat but with one blow of the hero's club the beast lay dead.

Now the giant approached and, at the sight of the monster's three heads, six arms and six legs as thick as tree trunks, even Heracles trembled. But he remembered that the Sun God was his friend, and with his bow he fired an arrow which flew through the air and hit the giant in the stomach where all three bodies met. The monster fell to the ground, the whole earth shook, and the giant was dead. Then Heracles drove the cattle down to the boat, even though it seemed too small to take them all. But as the cows got on board, the ship grew until there was room for the whole herd. Then the golden boat sailed off by itself and brought them all back to the land Heracles had left. Helios was waiting there and Heracles thanked him and gave back the boat.

As Heracles drove the cattle back towards Mycenae, the goddess Hera decided his task had been made far too easy so she sent a swarm of flies which stung the cattle and made them stampede in all directions. Heracles had to chase each one and it took a long time to gather the herd together again. But, at long last, the cattle of Helios, the Sun God, reached King Eurystheus' palace where they were given to the Temple of Hera.

28. Cerberus, the Hound of Hell

The next task King Eurystheus gave to Heracles was to fetch the Golden Apples of the Hesperides.

Far, far in the north, beyond the everlasting ice and snow, there was a valley with a garden full of flowers and fruit more beautiful than anything else on earth. In that garden was a tree that bore golden apples. The tree was guarded by four maidens called the Hesperides, and a dragon that had a hundred heads and never slept.

Heracles set out to find the garden, which was like paradise. Wherever he went he asked people for directions. Although everyone had heard of the garden no one knew where to find it. So Heracles travelled from land to land searching and asking. One day he came to the Caucasus mountains and found poor Prometheus chained to the rock. When Heracles asked how he could help, Prometheus said: "If someone is willing to give his life for mine, I can be set free." Then Heracles remembered the suffering Centaur Chiron and decided to go and find him.

The wise old Centaur gladly agreed to give up his life of pain. Even Zeus agreed that Prometheus could go free if the immortal Chiron gave up his life. So Chiron died and his suffering ended. Then Heracles went back to Prometheus and broke his chains. However Zeus had sworn Prometheus would be bound to the rock forever, and the King of the Gods could not break his word. So, after he was freed by Heracles, Prometheus had to wear a ring with a chip of the rock set in it, and in that way Zeus kept his word.

Heracles travelled on and came to a land where no human beings lived. In this lonely landscape he saw a giant standing on top of a mountain. The giant, a Titan called Atlas, carried the whole sky on his shoulders. The word atlas, the name of a book containing maps of the world, comes from this Titan Atlas.

Heracles spoke to Atlas and said: "I seek the golden apples from the Garden of the Hesperides. Tell me where I can find it."

The Titan answered: "I know where the garden is, for I am the only one who knows every place on earth. But I will help you even more. I will go and get the golden apples if, in the meantime, you stay here and hold up the sky for me."

Heracles agreed. He climbed the mountain and took the whole weight of the sky on his mighty shoulders. For three days and three nights Heracles carried the sky on his back. Then the giant returned with the golden apples. But he looked at Heracles and said: "I have had enough of carrying that heavy burden of the sky. I am leaving you to carry it while I go travelling. Farewell, Heracles."

Quickly Heracles answered: "Just a moment Atlas. I want to put a cushion on my back for my shoulders hurt. Just hold the sky up while I put the cushion in place."

But when Atlas took the sky back on his huge shoulders, Heracles said: "You are not clever enough to travel through the world. You must stay here and continue carrying the sky. Goodbye." And he left Atlas and took the apples back to King Eurystheus.

Now came the last labour, and King Eurystheus thought for a long time to find the most difficult task in the world. In the end he thought of something which would make even the bravest hero shudder. He said to Heracles: "Bring me the dog called Cerberus that guards the Underworld."

Heracles trembled with fear but Pallas Athene appeared to him and said: "When you have accomplished this task, there will be nothing in the world that can make you afraid." The goddess led him to a mountain range far away from any people, and showed him a cave which was the entrance to the Underworld. Heracles left Pallas Athene and walked into the cave where the Messenger God, Hermes, awaited him. Hermes guided him further and further into a dark tunnel which eventually opened out into a strange wide field. Everything was a colourless grey, and a deathly silence hung over the place. They walked on until they came to a river as black as ink. Without speaking a word, a ferryman rowed them across. On the other side Heracles saw misty shadows that were the ghosts of the dead.

Finally, Hermes led Heracles through a black gate into the palace of Hades, the King of the Underworld. Hades sat on his throne wearing a black robe embroidered with red flames. Heracles bowed before the king and told him why he had come. Hades replied: "I give you permission to take Cerberus if you can capture the dog without the use of weapons."

Heracles went in search of the terrible dog that had three heads growing from three necks, and a dragon's head at the end of its tail. When he found Cerberus, the dog barked and poison dripped from its fangs but Heracles wrapped his arms around the three necks and squeezed with all his strength. The dragon's head at the end of the tail bit Heracles' leg, but he squeezed harder, and the Hound of Hell recognized that it had found its master. When Heracles let go, Cerberus crouched before him and licked his feet.

Heracles put the dog on a rope and dragged the monster along behind him. Back they went: across the river; across the grey field; through the tunnel of darkness and into the cave. As Heracles pulled the dog out of the cave, Hermes left him. The daylight made Cerberus mad with fury. The monster barked and howled and wherever poison dripped from its mouth on to the earth, hemlock, a poisonous plant, grew. (Later, hemlock was used in Greece to execute criminals.)

When King Eurystheus heard that Heracles had accomplished the last task and was dragging Cerberus back on the end of a rope, he shook with fear. He sent his whole army to stop the hero from bringing the Hound of Hell into his palace. When Heracles met the army, he took out a knife and cut the rope. Then the earth opened under the dog and Cerberus leapt inside and disappeared.

At last Heracles was free again. Through his twelve great deeds he had cleansed himself of the killing of his children.

29. Heracles the Immortal

The Greek people admired Heracles for his twelve labours and when he came home he was greeted like a god. To show his gratitude to the gods who had helped him, Heracles built a city called Olympia in honour of the gods who live on Mount Olympus.

Every four years at Olympia there were contests to find the strongest and fastest men in Greece. Singers, poets and musicians also took part in competitions to find the best among them. The winners of the athletic events were given crowns of olive leaves and palm branches while the artists received crowns of laurel leaves as prizes. This was the highest honour a Greek could win and no victor would have exchanged his wreath of green leaves for either gold or gems.

While Heracles had been in the service of King Eurystheus performing his twelve labours, his first wife had died. Now he married Deianira, the daughter of a king. But Heracles was so used to a life of travel that he and his wife continued to wander about in search of adventure.

One day they came to the banks of a wide river, where a Centaur called Nessus lived. The Centaur carried travellers on his broad back across the river, but Heracles told him: "I don't need help to cross the river. I can wade through myself. But you can carry my wife across so that she does not get wet." And so Deianira sat on Nessus' back and the Centaur entered the water. Deianira was very beautiful and the Centaur began to wish he could have her for his own wife, so when they were in mid-stream he turned and began to gallop away. Deianira cried out and Heracles, who had already reached the other bank, saw what was happening. Quickly he fired an arrow from his bow. It hit the Centaur and he fell to the ground.

But as Nessus lay dying he planned his revenge. He said to

Deianira: "As you are the last person I have carried on my back, I
want to make you a gift. Collect the blood which flows from my
wound and use it to dye a tunic for Heracles. If ever your husband
becomes weak, let him wear the tunic and it will restore his
strength." Then the Centaur died. Deianira believed this treacherous advice and collected the blood from the wound in a cup.
Secretly she dyed one of Heracles' tunics and hid it away. But
Deianira did not know that the Centaur's blood was poisoned by
the blood of the Hydra that Heracles used on the tips of his arrows.

Later Heracles fought in a war against a cruel, evil king. He
and his friends gained a great victory, but when the hero
returned from the battle Deianira thought he looked haggard
and tired. He was not exhausted but looked ill because he had a
strange feeling that he was going to die very soon. Deianira
thought he was losing his strength and went off to find the
tunic. While Heracles prepared a sacrifice to the gods to thank
them for victory, Deianira gave the garment to a servant. She
said: "Tell Heracles to wear this tunic for the sacrifice. I had it
made specially for him to celebrate the victory."

Heracles was very pleased with the red tunic. He put it on and
kindled the fire on the altar. But as the flames on the altar flick-
ered, the tunic felt as if it were burning inside. Roaring with pain,
Heracles wanted to tear the tunic from his body but it was as if it
had grown to his skin. Deianira came, crying bitterly, and told her
husband what had happened. Heracles forgave her for she had
not meant any harm. But no ointment or herbs could soothe the
pains which racked Heracles and he knew that he was dying.

At his command he was carried to the peak of a mountain
and there a great heap of wood was piled up. With his last ounce
of strength Heracles climbed on top and one of his friends set
fire to it. The flames roared, and it seemed to the people who
watched that a great eagle emerged from the smoke and soared
higher and higher until it could not be seen any more.

Heracles was welcomed by Zeus as one of the gods, and even
Hera, the wife of Zeus, was no longer his enemy. And so, just as
it had been prophesied when he was a child, Heracles joined the
ranks of the gods that live on Mount Olympus.

Theseus

30. The Labyrinth of Minos

Greece is a warm and sunny country. The winter is short and most of the year there is dazzling sun and a blue sky which is reflected in the deep blue waters of the Aegean Sea. The country includes hundreds of islands, some big and some small, some near the mainland, some further away. And the largest of the islands is called Crete. Today, many farmers and shepherds live on Crete. Four thousand years ago the island of Crete was a rich and mighty kingdom.

Some years ago, the people on Crete were very surprised when learned men who studied history came and dug up the earth in many places on the island. They were even more surprised when the ruins of houses and palaces that had been built by the Cretan people long ago were uncovered. These buildings from the past were often three or four storeys high. The walls had been decorated with wonderful paintings and some of the roofs had once had gardens on them. The paintings on the walls show that the most popular sport at that time was the "bull dance." Young girls and boys, about sixteen or seventeen years old, are pictured somersaulting over a bull's back.

Although the unearthed palace of the King of Crete was mostly in ruins, it was still possible to see that it had once been enormous. It contained chapels for the worship of gods, workshops for skilled craftsmen who made beautiful vases, jewellery and urns, and huge storerooms where food for hundreds of people could be kept. At that time Crete was a wealthy country and the people were rich merchants and brave sailors. Their ships sailed to countries far and near carrying things the craftsmen made and returned laden with silver, tin and copper.

The kings of Crete were very powerful. Not only did they rule the island of Crete itself, but many of the smaller islands as well. And even cities on the mainland of Greece, for instance

Athens, had to pay tribute to the King of Crete by sending him goods, usually olive oil and wheat.

One of the rich and powerful kings was called Minos. One day King Minos made a promise to Poseidon, the God of the Sea. There was a great storm at sea and King Minos promised he would sacrifice his most beautiful bull to Poseidon if his fleet came back safely. The next day the sea was calm again and the king's fleet returned unharmed. But Minos was mean and although he did sacrifice a bull, it was the poorest and scraggliest of beasts. Poseidon was furious and cursed King Minos for his meanness. Not long after that something terrible happened. The king's wife was expecting a child but, when she gave birth, the baby had a human body and a bull's head.

Now, at the court of King Minos lived a clever Greek called Daedalus who was very good at designing and making things.* (Today we would call somebody like Daedalus who draws plans and designs things an engineer.) One day King Minos said to Daedalus: "I want you to make something very special for me. I want you to build a maze that is so complicated that nobody will find their way out." So Daedalus sat down and designed a maze. He planned a building that would be divided by many walls, and the paths between the walls would twist and turn in every direction. Many other paths would branch off so that anyone who entered the maze would very soon be lost. The building was to be called the Labyrinth and the only person who would know the way out was Daedalus himself.

The Labyrinth took many years to build, and, in the meantime, the monster with a bull's head that had been born to King Minos, grew up. The poor creature was not only very ugly to look at, but it had also developed the horrible habit of eating human beings. It had already killed and devoured many servants at the palace. The people of Crete were very afraid of the monster, which was known as the Minotaur or the Bull of Minos.

---

* It is worth pointing out that Daedalus had fled to Crete from Athens having been condemned by the Areopagus for the murder of his nephew, Talus, who had invented the potter's wheel and the saw. This makes the death of his son Icarus (see p. 102) perhaps more obviously a case of Divine justice. P.S.

Finally, when the Labyrinth was finished, the king had the Minotaur taken right into the centre of the building. Then he demanded that the islands and cities that paid tribute send him young men and maidens. These young people were driven into the Labyrinth, and after getting lost in the maze they were eaten up by the monster.

Daedalus was horrified at the use King Minos made of his building. He wanted to leave Crete but the king said: "No, I don't want anyone else to have a labyrinth. You cannot leave. You must stay here on the island." And, as all the ships that came to Crete obeyed the king's will, Daedalus could find no way to escape. But one day as he sat sadly with his young son Icarus, Daedalus thought of a very clever way of escaping from cruel King Minos.

31. Flight to Freedom

Daedalus had a plan to escape from the island of Crete with his son Icarus. They could not go by ship, for no sea captain would dare disobey the king who had forbidden father and son to leave. Now, for a long time Daedalus had been watching birds in flight and his plan was to make two pairs of wings. No man had ever tried to fly before but Daedalus was sure that his plan would work. So father and son began to gather all the birds' feathers they could find and kept them hidden in a chest. One day in the hills of Crete they found an eagle which had been killed by a hunter's arrow. They took the wing-feathers home and added them to their collection. Then Daedalus decided they had enough and, using beeswax to stick the feathers together, he made two pairs of large, strong wings. When they were finished he put straps on them so that they could be attached to the arms.

Now everything was ready. But before they took off, Daedalus told young Icarus: "You must never fly too high. If you do the heat of the sun will melt the wax that holds the feathers together. But neither must you fly too low, for the wings must not touch water." Icarus promised to follow his father's advice. And so, one morning when Minos and his courtiers were still asleep, Daedalus and his son strapped on their wings and flew away.

They soon left Crete far behind as they winged their way through the air. Mindful that it was only wax that held the wing-feathers together, Daedalus did not fly very high. But young Icarus rejoiced in the lift of the great sweeping wings, and he quickly forgot his father's warning. Higher and higher he soared until he seemed only a little dot in the heights. By then it was noon; the sun shone with great heat and slowly the wax holding Icarus' wings together began to melt like butter. The feathers started to fall out and it was not long before Icarus plunged into the sea and drowned.

In great sorrow Daedalus continued his flight alone. He landed before nightfall on the island of Sicily and carried his wings to the Temple of Apollo. There he left them as a gift to the God of the Sun Rays. He soon found work with the King of Sicily but, although he had escaped from the cruel King Minos, Daedalus often grieved for the son he had lost.

Back in Crete, Minos was furious that Daedalus had escaped. But there was nothing he could do, and anyway he still had the Labyrinth and the terrible monster, the Minotaur, that lived in it.* And the islands and cities that owed him tribute continued to send young men and women to feed the beast.

One of the Greek cities which had to pay King Minos tribute was Athens. Once a year, the seven most handsome youths and the seven most beautiful maidens from the city were put on a ship to Crete to be devoured by the Minotaur. It was a sad day for the parents of these young people; it was a sad day for the whole of Athens when the best of their youth set out on a journey from which there was no return. But the time was near when a hero would come to the rescue and make an end to this shameful tribute.

Now the King of Athens at that time was called Aegeus. He was already an elderly man and could not have gone to war against the powerful kingdom of Crete. However, when Aegeus was a young prince he had travelled through the Greek islands. And on the island of Troezen he had met and married a beautiful princess called Aethra. But there was an ancient law on Troezen which prevented women born on the island from leaving, so when Aegeus had to return to Athens, his wife, Princess Aethra, could not follow him. But she had given birth to a little boy called Theseus, and this was her comfort when Aegeus left.

And so little Theseus grew up on the island without a father. His mother looked after him and even as a boy he showed that he was fearless. One day the great hero Heracles visited Troezen. Now you remember that Heracles always wore the skin of a lion over his shoulder. As Heracles sat down to a meal

---

* According to Herodotus, Minos pursued Daedalus to Sicily, where the Cretan King met with a violent death. P.S.

the hospitable Princess Aethra had prepared for him, he threw the lion skin with its gaping jaws over a chair. Just then Theseus and a crowd of other children came in, but when the children saw the lion's head they cried out in fear and ran away. But not little Theseus. Snatching an axe, he attacked the lion's head. Heracles laughed and showed the boy that it was really only the skin of a lion. Later Heracles said to his mother: "One day this son of yours will be a hero as famous as I am."

32. The Road to Athens

Now before Aegeus had left Troezen he had buried his royal sword under a great rock. Often, while Theseus was growing up, Princess Aethra would take him to the place where the sword was hidden. She told Theseus that as soon as he was strong enough to lift the rock he could claim his rightful place as the son of the King of Athens. Theseus grew up to be a strong young man, and on the day he turned twenty-one he managed to lift the rock and claim the sword his father, Aegeus, had left for him.

Theseus was sad that the time had come to leave his mother. But he was eager to meet his father and, above all, he longed for adventure. He said goodbye to Aethra and set out by boat for the Greek mainland. Theseus could have sailed straight to Athens, but he preferred to make the last part of his journey by land. He had heard that robbers and giants lived in that part of the country and he was eager to meet danger.

Soon he came to a steep cliff rising straight out of the sea. On top of the cliff a cruel bandit named Sciron had his stronghold. Sciron used to sit on a rock on the cliff top and force passing travellers to wash his feet. But as they stooped down, the bandit would kick them over the cliff into the sea far below. As Theseus approached, the bandit called out: "Come here and wash my feet, or you will die by my sword."

"I will do this little service for you with pleasure," answered Theseus. He bent down and quickly lifted Sciron by his feet and threw him over the cliff. And so the bandit drowned in the sea, as his poor victims had died before him.

Further on there was another brute called Sinis. He was very strong, so strong that he could bend the tops of pine trees right down to the ground. Capturing passing travellers, he tied them to the bent trees by their arms and legs. When the trees were released the poor victim was torn to pieces. Theseus wrestled Sinis to the ground and tied him to two bent trees so that he suffered the same fate as his many victims.

Theseus continued his journey and met up with a giant, called Procrustes, who often invited travellers to spend a night in his house. With a wicked smile, he would show his guest to the bed and say: "You must be tired. Lie down on the bed, my friend, and see if it is the right length for you." Now if the bed was too long, the giant held the traveller's head and feet and stretched them to fit and, of course, under that treatment they died. If, however, a guest was too tall, Procrustes would shorten him by cutting his legs off with an axe. In this way the giant had killed many people and he planned to play the same trick on Theseus. Procrustes led Theseus to the bed and said: "Lie down. Let's see if it is the right size for you."

"I would rather see how you fit in the bed," Theseus replied, as he grabbed the giant in his iron grasp. He forced Procrustes down and tied him to the bed. Then Theseus said: "I see you are too tall for the bed," and he picked up the giant's axe and cut his head off in one stroke.

In this way Theseus overcame the cruel men and evil monsters who had made the journey to Athens so dangerous. On the day Theseus arrived in the city, he heard that there was to be a great banquet at the king's palace. He slipped in to join the crowd and sat down at a table. A huge piece of meat was being passed round and the guests carved slices off with their knives. But there was great surprise when the meat came to Theseus. He did not use a knife but drew out his sword to slice the meat. King Aegeus stared with amazement at the young man and wondered who he was. Then he recognized the sword as his own and cried out: "Theseus, my son. My son has come!" Father and son embraced and there was great joy.

But the next day King Aegeus said to Theseus: "My dear son, you have come at a time of sorrow. Tomorrow Athens will lose seven of its most handsome young men and seven of its most beautiful maidens." Then he told Theseus about King Minos, and the Labyrinth where the Minotaur lived.

But brave Theseus said: "I will put an end to this. I will go with them myself as one of the seven young men." So he planned to set out with the doomed youths and maidens to the island of Crete.

33. Ariadne's Thread

King Aegeus was very unhappy. His son had only just arrived at the palace and now he had offered himself as one of the fourteen young Athenians to be devoured by the Minotaur. He tried to persuade his son to stay, but Theseus would not listen.

Now, the ships that took the doomed youths from Athens to Crete hoisted black sails as a sign of mourning. And when Theseus went aboard and bade farewell to his father, King Aegeus said to him: "Promise me one thing, my son. If the gods favour you and you really can save yourself and the others, hoist a white sail on your return journey so that I can see from afar that all is well. But if the ship comes back carrying black sails, I shall know that I have lost my son and Athens has lost another fourteen of her children." And Theseus promised faithfully that he would hoist a white sail if all went well.

So the ship sailed away to the island of Crete. When it arrived, King Minos and his whole court were at the port. The king had come to make sure that the Athenians had really sent the most handsome of their young folk. This time he could not complain; the victims were good looking indeed, especially one of them who had a truly royal bearing and called himself Theseus. King Minos' daughter, Ariadne, was also waiting at the harbour. When she saw the tall, handsome Theseus, she fell in love with him and decided to help him escape the terrible monster in the Labyrinth.

The Athenians were not taken straight to the Minotaur. Instead they were led to the palace, given a meal and then each one was sent to a separate room to get a good night's sleep. King Minos wanted them to be well rested when they went into the Labyrinth, so that the monster would have real sport with them.

But at night, when everyone was asleep in the palace, the king's daughter crept soundlessly to the room where Theseus lay. She said to him: "Noble Athenian, I have come to rescue you from a horrible fate in the Labyrinth. I will help you, but you must promise to take me with you to Athens for my father would kill me if he finds out I have helped you."

Theseus answered: "Beautiful princess, I shall gladly take you with me."

Ariadne then gave him a magic sword — the only one that could kill the Minotaur — and a ball of thread, and said: "Tie the end of the thread to the door-post at the entrance of the Labyrinth. As you go along the passages let the ball unwind and then, when you have dealt with the Minotaur, you can follow the thread out again."

As soon as Ariadne left, Theseus slipped silently from his room and hurried to the Labyrinth. The entrance was like a black, gaping mouth but he was not afraid. He tied the end of the thread to the door-post, just as the princess had said, and strode into the darkness. He held the ball loosely in his left hand, so that it could unwind, and the sword in his right hand. If it had not been for the thread, Theseus would soon have been lost in the dark twisting passages. Then he heard the roaring and bellowing of the Minotaur; it had smelt a human being approaching and was getting ready to attack. Theseus put the ball of thread down by his feet so that he could easily find it again in the dark, and tightened his hand on the sword. Then, a huge ink-black shadow loomed before him and he could feel the monster's hot breath. Theseus put out his left hand and caught hold of a horn. With iron strength he pulled the Minotaur's head down and, with a swift stroke of the sword, cut right through its neck. The creature collapsed and Theseus picked up his ball of thread and followed it back to the entrance.

It was still dark when Theseus returned from the Labyrinth. Quickly he went round to wake his comrades and Princess Ariadne and told them what had happened. They all stole away from the palace and through the silent, sleepy streets to the harbour. Their ship was waiting and the Athenian crew rowed quickly away. And when morning came, King Minos found that not only was the Minotaur dead and the prisoners gone, but that his daughter had vanished as well.

34. Success and Sorrow

The Greeks believed that with every happiness the gods always mixed a little unhappiness to stop human beings getting too haughty and conceited. It was certainly so with Theseus and his companions; the joy of their escape was to be mixed with sorrow. And this is how it happened.

On the return voyage to Athens they saw a storm coming and sailed to the little island of Naxos for shelter. Now, as you have heard, Ariadne, the daughter of King Minos, had fallen in love with Theseus. But the gods had other plans; she was meant to become the wife of Dionysus, the God of Wine. While the Athenians rested on the island, Dionysus appeared to Theseus in a dream and said: "Ariadne is not for you; no mortal man shall be her husband. You must sail from this island without her."

When Theseus and his friends woke, they found that Ariadne was in such a deep sleep that nothing could rouse her. Then Theseus told them his dream and, fearing the anger of the gods, they left Ariadne and sailed away. When, at long last, the princess woke and found that Theseus had deserted her, she wept bitter tears. But Dionysus appeared and comforted her, and in the end she became his bride.

Meanwhile, Theseus and his ship had almost reached Athens. But the Athenians were so happy to have survived that the promise to hoist a white sail if all went well was forgotten. So, as the boat approached the harbour, it was still carrying the black sails with which it had set out.

Now, every day King Aegeus stood on a steep rock on the shore watching for the white sails that would tell him that his son was safe. At long last he saw in the distance the ship that he knew so well; the ship that had carried so many Athenians to their death. There it was on the horizon, but it carried the black sails of doom. When the king saw those dark sails he cried out in despair and threw himself into the sea where he drowned. Ever since, the sea on the east of Greece has been called the Aegean.

Once again unhappiness was mixed with happiness and when the ship reached port, Theseus learnt that his own forgetfulness had caused his father's death. But the Athenians hailed him and cheered him, for he had brought back their children and overcome the Minotaur. And Theseus became King of Athens.

He was a fair and just king. But he found that the Athenians quarrelled among themselves endlessly so he appointed judges, wise men who would decide who was right and who was wrong when there was an argument. Then Theseus ordered that a great building, a house of justice or a law court, be built as a special place where quarrels could be settled.

The Athenians held Theseus in great respect, and long after he died they said that his spirit still watched over their city. Many hundreds of years later, when a powerful enemy invaded Greece and threatened Athens, there was a great battle. The Athenians said that the spirit of Theseus fought by their side, fully armed, and that only through his help had they gained victory.

Greek History

35. A Royal Sacrifice

In ancient times Greece was divided into many cities and each one was like a country on its own. Even though the Greeks all spoke the same language — a very beautiful language — every city had its own laws, its own customs, its own kings and rulers, its own army and its own fleet of ships. Every Greek was immensely proud of his city and ready to fight for it. And it happened quite often that one city went to war with another.

You have heard how Theseus became king of the city of Athens in ancient Greece. Now many years after Theseus died, Athens was ruled by one of his descendants called Codrus. And when Codrus was king, a city called Megara went to war against Athens. Megara had many more soldiers than Athens and, in the first battle, although the Athenians fought bravely, they were defeated. King Codrus realized that Athens was not strong enough to win the war, and he did not know what he could do to save his beloved city.

Now in ancient Greece people went to the Oracle of Delphi for advice. We heard about the oracle in the story of Heracles; how a priestess sat in the temple on a three-legged chair over a cleft in the earth. Smoke rose through the cleft and every word the priestess said was regarded as coming from the god Apollo. Delphi was a holy city and no Greek would ever have gone to war against it. It was the only city which never had to fight a war.

So Codrus, the King of Athens, went to Delphi to ask the oracle how his city could be saved. And the priestess said: "Athens will be destroyed if King Codrus lives. But if King Codrus is killed by the enemy, by the soldiers of Megara, then Athens will be saved."

Now Codrus was a brave man and he was ready to give his life to save Athens. But, as it turned out, this was not so easy. The soldiers of Megara got to hear of the prophecy, and when the king took part in the next battle they refused to fight him. However, they fought all the other Athenians around him and once again the soldiers of Athens were defeated. King Codrus had to flee with them, or he would have been taken prisoner.

So you see, Codrus was willing to give up his life yet he could not get himself killed in battle. But he loved Athens and wanted to save his city, so he thought of a plan to fool the enemy. Disguised as a peasant he carried fruit into the enemy camp to sell to the soldiers. After one of the soldiers had bought and paid for some fruit, Codrus cried out: "Hey, you rogue, you have not paid me." The soldier was furious and said: "I have paid you, and don't you call me names." But the king shouted: "You, and all men of Megara, are nothing but thieves and robbers!" Now the other soldiers became angry and told him to leave. But the king only got wilder. He cursed them, and then picked up a big stick and hit one of the soldiers so hard that he fell down dead. That was too much for the soldiers and they drew their swords. There was a brief fight and the peasant fell down bleeding, and soon died of his wounds. Only then did the soldiers see that under the peasant's rags, the dead man wore a royal purple robe. Horrified, they realized that they had killed King Codrus. They remembered the oracle's prophecy and were so disheartened that they gave up the war and went back to Megara.

The people of Athens were grateful to King Codrus for saving their city. Codrus had no children and the Athenians thought there was no one worthy enough to become king after him. But a city must have someone to rule over it and the people decided that they would chose nine men who would rule together for a year. The following year another nine men, or archons, would be elected. In this way the people of Athens became the first to elect their government. For the first time in history there was no king but a government chosen by the people — which is called a democracy.

36. Spartan Warriors

Greece was not one country under one ruler, but was divided into many city states, each with its own government, army and fleet. A city state was not only the city itself, but also the countryside around it. Now the two most important cities in Greece were Athens and Sparta. But life in Athens and life in Sparta were utterly different; just as different as summer and winter.

First let us turn to life in Sparta. We heard about Menelaus, the King of Sparta who was married to Helen. And the great hero Heracles was specially admired by the Spartans, as Theseus was specially remembered in Athens. The laws of Sparta had been worked out by a wise man called Lycurgus. He had travelled through many foreign countries studying their rules and customs, which is why the people of Sparta asked him to make their laws.

Lycurgus and his fellow Spartans thought that there was only one task worthy of a man — and that was fighting. If you had shown a Spartan a beautiful painting or talked about poetry or science, he would have looked at you with contempt, and said: "That's all nonsense! A man should be interested in making his muscles strong, in practising with sword and spear to become a better and better fighter. Everything else is just a waste of time!" Even work was shameful for a Spartan. All the workers, from the farmers to the carpenters and the cobblers, were slaves. A Spartan would, however, build his own house but his real work was fighting, or training for fighting, and nothing else. So, because the Spartans believed that fighting was the only thing worth doing, the laws which Lycurgus made had only one purpose: to make every Spartan boy a fierce warrior.

Every baby born in Sparta was brought before a council who decided if the child would be strong and healthy or weak and sickly. If the poor baby looked weak, then the council gave the order: "Take that weakling into the mountains and leave it there on a rock to die." The mother and father had no say in this at all and the babies were taken to a wild place called Mount Taygetus. If the child was healthy it was allowed to stay at home only until the age of seven. When a boy reached that age he was taken from his family and put into a military school where he lived until he turned twenty one.

Life was hard in these military schools. There were no beds; the boys had to sleep on the bare floor on reeds from the riverbank. They had to gather the rushes with their bare hands — knives were not allowed. Food was scarce and the boys were always hungry. If they wanted more food they were told to steal it. But if a boy was caught stealing he was given a merciless whipping, not for stealing, but for getting caught.

The boys were taught to endure pain by being given a severe flogging for the smallest thing. If you showed you were tired after a long march or some gym exercise you were flogged, for it was shameful to show any signs of pain. Once a Spartan boy hid a stolen fox cub under his tunic. The fox bit into him but the boy showed no sign of pain. At last the fox bit so deep that the boy fell down dead, but he had never uttered a cry.

In both summer and winter the boys wore the same thin tunic. Every day they spent hours and hours doing gymnastics. They ran and jumped, practised with swords and spears, and marched. But they had to do all this in the open air — no matter if it was hot or cold, or whether there was rain or wind or snow. To make themselves warm they rubbed their bodies hard with sand and oil.

Both Spartan men and women were brought up to speak as little as possible. They did not gossip and chatter to one another. And when they spoke, they said in a few words what other people could only say if they spoke at length.

There is a story about a young Spartan soldier who came to say goodbye to his mother before going to war. She pointed to his shield and simply said: "With it, or upon it." What did she mean? You see, when a soldier in ancient Greece fled the battlefield, he would throw away his heavy shield so he could run faster. If you came back "with it", with the shield, it showed you had not run away but fought bravely. But if a soldier was killed his comrades carried the body back "upon it", that is, upon the shield. So what the Spartan mother really said was: "Fight bravely, never run away, even if it costs your life." Instead she said it in five words: "With it, or upon it." You can also see from this story that the women of Sparta were as tough as the men. They would sooner see their sons dead than coming back alive but as cowards.

But life was not easy for the adults in Sparta either. No one in Sparta could do as they pleased for their lives were controlled by strict rules and laws. For instance:

Every Spartan had to marry at the age of thirty — not before and not after.

Each man had to build his own house using nothing but an axe and a saw.

At night no lights were allowed in streets or houses so that, in a war, the Spartans would be trained to see in the dark.

No Spartan family had its own kitchen or was allowed to choose its own food. Every fourteen families had a community kitchen where the same very plain food was cooked by slaves for all of them.

No one was allowed to own any gold or silver. The Spartans thought these were luxuries that would only make people soft. And the only money they had were coins of iron.

And the Spartans themselves were people like iron — hard, tough and fearless. They were not men of words but men of deeds.

37. Athenian Orators

Sparta and Athens were as different as winter and summer. The Spartans had kings, two kings who ruled side by side. And every Spartan was brought up to obey these kings without question. But the Athenians, as we heard, elected their rulers and could change these archons every year.

The Athenians also had a lawgiver like the Spartan Lycurgus. His name was Solon but he was quite different from Lycurgus. Solon and his fellow Athenians loved beauty. In fact, to this day no other nation has had such a love for beauty and made such beautiful things as the people of ancient Athens.

When Athenians put on their robes they took great care that every fold lay the right way. And there was not a jar or a pot or a pan in an Athenian house that was not beautifully made. On a hill called the Acropolis in the middle of the city the Athenians built a great temple to the goddess Pallas Athene. There were many other temples too with shining marble pillars and beautiful statues made of ivory and gold. And the city streets were lined with many other statues of gods, goddesses and heroes.

Unlike the Spartans, the Athenians loved to talk. Even in day-to-day conversation they spoke beautifully, as people nowadays would speak on the stage in a theatre. The art of speaking is called eloquence and the Athenians admired eloquence. To speak crudely or carelessly would have been shameful for an Athenian. What was said had to be clever and beautiful, and they loved to listen to people who could speak well.

Children had a much easier life in Athens than in Sparta. Athenian children could live with their parents although they also had to do a lot of gymnastic exercises. All Greeks wanted to make their bodies strong and healthy. But the Athenian boys and girls did their gymnastics in the open only when it was a sunny day. When it was cold their teachers took them into the gymnasium to practice eloquence. They also learnt many poems: the poems of

Homer, poems about the Trojan War and the adventures of Odysseus. To recite a poem well, to tell a story so that it was a pleasure to listen, was the pride of any Athenian boy or girl. The Spartans thought that a man should only train to fight. But the Athenians were skilled craftsmen and artists. They were also clever traders, merchants and businessmen and their ships sailed the seas, bringing wealth to the city.

Solon, the lawgiver of Athens, was at first a businessman. He travelled to foreign countries on business and was often away for many years. One day when he returned after a long absence, he found his fellow citizens sad and downcast. They had just lost another war against Megara and paid a large sum of gold to that city to be left in peace. The Athenians were so ashamed that the nine archons had made a law forbidding people to speak about the war. Of course people did speak about it, but only in whispers.

Now, right in the centre of Athens there was a great square called the Agora where the Athenians came to talk and to listen to public speakers. In those days there were no newspapers or television sets and if the government had made a new law or wanted to make an announcement, speakers went to the Agora to address the people.

When Solon heard about the lost war and the silly law that no one must talk about it, he went straight to the Agora. There were raised steps in various places in the Agora where speakers could stand, so that they were a little above the listeners. Such a step was called a rostrum, and if you mounted a rostrum it meant you had something to say and people crowded round to listen.

Solon mounted a rostrum, a crowd soon gathered, and he began to speak about the war against Megara. But he did not break the law, for he did not speak in the ordinary way. Instead he recited a beautiful poem calling on the people to take up arms again and defeat their old enemy. The Athenians were so moved by his poem that they went into battle again and conquered Megara once and for all. After that the Athenians made Solon their only archon and lawgiver.

So you see what power a beautiful speech or poem had in Athens. Such a thing could never have happened in Sparta.

38. A Slave for an Eye

In Sparta it was Lycurgus who made the laws that produced tough, fierce, warriors. But when Lycurgus first made these laws, not all Spartans were pleased. There were some rich men in the city who, because of their wealth, enjoyed all kinds of luxury. And these rich people were not pleased when they heard that they would have to give up their soft beds, fancy food and beautiful clothes. The rich men thought these laws were unfair. One day as Lycurgus was walking through the streets they gathered around him shouting angrily and cursing him. One of them, called Alkandros, hit Lycurgus in the face with a stick and knocked out an eye. When the others saw what had happened they were ashamed and handed Alkandros to the lawmaker saying he could do what he liked with him.

Now Lycurgus, in true Spartan fashion, had not uttered a word when he was attacked. And after Alkandros had been handed over to him he said simply: "Come with me." Alkandros followed Lycurgus to his house. Although he was terrified at the thought of the punishment that would follow the loss of an eye, Alkandros was too much of a Spartan to think of running away.

When they reached the house, Lycurgus called all his servants and slaves and told them that they were now free. After the slaves left Lycurgus said to Alkandros: "You had better put a bandage on the eye you knocked out." Alkandros did so with trembling fingers. Lycurgus then told him to prepare a meal, and when that was done he found him other household tasks to do.

And that was Alkandros' punishment; to became Lycurgus' servant. And he became a most faithful servant who loved and praised his master. Then the day came when Lycurgus had given all his laws to Sparta. He asked the Spartans to swear an oath not to change his laws until he returned from a long journey. The oath was sworn and Lycurgus and the faithful Alkandros left Sparta. But they never returned and no one ever discovered where they went. The Spartans, however, kept their oath and their children continued to go to military schools where they became fearless warriors.

39. The Sunlight Tree

The story of how Lycurgus dealt with the man who knocked out one of his eyes, and the story of Solon, the lawgiver of Athens, inspiring the Athenians by reciting a poem to fight and conquer Megara shows again the difference between the two cities: the Athenians admired Solon because of his eloquence while the Spartans admired Lycurgus because of his deed. The Spartan had not spoken much but he acted wisely and generously.

Now it is not hard to guess that the city of Athens is named after the Goddess of Wisdom, Pallas Athene. Athens was under the special protection of Pallas Athene and there is a story of how this came about.

Long, long ago, long before Solon or Codrus or even Theseus, there were only a few fishermen's huts in the place where Athens would later be built. But as time went by, more and more people arrived and made their homes there. When it reached the size of a small town, the people decided the time had come to give it a name. And they decided that they would name their town after the god or goddess who made them the most valuable gift.

Now there were two gods who wanted to become the protector of the new city. One of them was the Sea God, Poseidon, the other was Pallas Athene, and they competed for the honour. Poseidon was the first to offer a gift to the new city. He struck a rock with his three-pronged spear called a trident, and out sprang a beautiful white horse. The people of the new city thought this was a wonderful gift, and some of them said: "Let us call our city Poseidonia. Poseidon is a great god; he will protect our ships at sea and he has given us this wonderful horse!" But others cried out: "No, let us wait for the present Pallas Athene will give us."

When Pallas Athene came she struck the ground with her spear and instantly a tree sprang up. But it was neither very beautiful nor very large. The branches and trunk were gnarled while the dull greyish-green leaves were small and spear shaped. Then people noticed that the tree bore fruit but, quite unlike red apples or golden oranges, this fruit looked like a small, hard green plum. And the people of the new city were not very impressed.

But then Pallas Athene said: "This is an olive tree. It will grow on rocky, hard soil and thrive in hot weather when the warmth of the sun will enter the fruit. But it will not make the fruit sweet and juicy. Instead the sun's light and heat will make the juice of the fruit into golden olive oil. And olive oil is so nourishing," said Pallas Athene, "that a poor farmer who cannot afford meat can eat a handful of olives and it will be just as sustaining as meat."

The goddess paused, then continued: "You can press the oil from the fruit and use it for cooking and, in a warm country like Greece, the oil will never go bad, or rancid as butter does. But you can also use the sunlight which is hidden in the olive oil in another way. You can fill little boat-shaped saucers with the oil and float a linen wick in it. If you light the wick you then have a lamp to bring a little bit of sunlight into your dark houses at night. And there is yet another thing you can do with it. When your young men practice gymnastics, they can rub their bodies with the oil and it will make their muscles supple and smooth. So you see," Pallas Athene said, "the sunlight which lives in the olive oil gives you four blessings."

The people realized what a wonderful gift the tree was. They chose Pallas Athene as protector and called their city Athenae, that is Athens, in her honour. And later, when Athens was a flourishing and wealthy city, they built a great temple to the goddess. And the most famous artist of the time, the sculptor Phidias, made a statue of Pallas Athene out of ivory and gold.

Today the olive tree is still an important source of food in Greece. In the old days the little lamps full of olive oil provided the only light there was at night. The wise men of Greece wrote their books by the light from these lamps, and the great emperors of Rome had no other light.

But there is something else. Because it is the sunlight itself which goes into the olive tree, the olive branch has always been the sign for peace. In the story of Heracles you read about the Olympic Games where Greeks met to test their strength and skill against each other. The city of Olympia was a holy place which was never attacked, and where people from every city met in peace. And they gave each other olive leaves as the sign of peace.

40. Hippias the Cruel Tyrant

When Solon became the lawmaker of Athens, there was a very good reason why the city needed someone to make new and just laws at that time. Athens had grown very rich. The beautiful things made by craftsmen, the oil from olive trees and many other goods were carried by Athenian ships and sold profitably in other lands.

However not all Athenians grew wealthy; some remained poor. So the poor Athenians often had to borrow money from the rich. But sometimes the poor could not repay the money and the rich would take their houses or plots of land instead. This forced the poor to become homeless beggars and sometimes even slaves of the rich.

The poor people of Athens did not like this state of affairs at all and fights and arguments broke out. But the rich Athenians remained powerful, yet both rich and poor realized that the fighting could, sooner or later, destroy their city. So they asked Solon to make laws that would bring peace to all the citizens of Athens.

The first thing that Solon did was to cancel all debts. That meant that all the poor who owed money to the rich did not have to pay it back. Solon also said that the people who had become slaves had to be set free, and the rich had to pay taxes which could be used to help a poor person in need.

Solon's laws brought peace and the Athenians were so grateful that they asked him to rule the city for the rest of his life. But Solon refused and said: "I warn you Athenians against ever allowing one man to rule your city. Such a man would be a tyrant, he could do just what he liked and you would lose the freedom to chose other rulers if you were not satisfied. Athens would no longer be a democracy." So Solon became an ordinary citizen and, once again, the Athenians had to chose nine men to become archons.

Solon had warned the Athenians that if they allowed just
one person to rule the city that person would become a tyrant.
In our time the word tyrant means an evil ruler or a cruel
master. But in ancient Greece a tyrant was a man who made
himself ruler without any right to rule such as a king or a
prince had. And when Solon was an old man, a tyrant did
come to power in Athens. His name was Pisistratus and he
seized power in a very cunning way. First he told the poor
people of Athens that the rich were planning to enslave and
oppress them again. Then Pisistratus offered to protect them.
But for this he would need a bodyguard of armed men to prevent the rich from killing him. But as soon as he had his
armed bodyguard, Pisistratus used it to chase out the council
of nine archons, and then he said: "From now on I am the
ruler of Athens and no one else."

It was a trick and the Athenians could do nothing because
Pisistratus' soldiers were ready to kill anybody who resisted or
would not obey. Yet he was, on the whole, a good tyrant. He
treated old Solon with great respect and did not change the laws
he had made. In fact, while Pisistratus lived Athens flourished
and grew even richer.

When Pisistratus died he was followed by his son Hippias.
However Hippias was not clever like his father. Pisistratus
had used his power wisely and had been a just ruler. But
Hippias was an evil tyrant who did not hesitate to put to death
anybody who spoke too freely against him. Now the
Athenians had put up with the first tyrant, Pisistratus, because
his rule had not been too harsh and their city had prospered.
But they were not willing to put up with Hippias who
oppressed them and was cruel. So the Athenians decided to
rebel. Hippias, who was too much of a coward to lead his
bodyguard into battle, fled, and Athens was free to choose its
own rulers again.

But this was not the end of Hippias. After he fled from
Athens he went to a great and mighty king, a king who had for
a long time planned to make himself master not only of
Athens but of the whole of Greece. His name was Darius, and
he was the King of Persia. Hippias hoped that when Persia

conquered Greece King Darius would make him the ruler of Athens again. So Pisistratus' son, Hippias, was quite willing to try and regain the power he had lost with the help of the Persians, who were the enemies of Athens and the whole of Greece.

41. The Wrath of Darius

The sea on the east coast of Greece is called the Aegean, after King Aegeus drowned there, and if you sail across this sea today, you come to the land of Turkey. But at the time when Solon made his wise laws, Greek merchants and sailors had built a number of cities on the coast, which was called Ionia. And these cities, which you could call colonies of Athens, flourished and grew rich.

But, in time, these Greek cities roused the envy and greed of a powerful neighbour, King Darius of Persia. His army had conquered one country after another and Babylon, Egypt and other smaller countries had all been swallowed up. So Persia was no longer a little kingdom but an enormous mighty empire twenty times bigger than Greece.

Darius, the King of Persia, just could not bear the thought that these Greek cities on the coast, which were next to his own territory, were not part of his vast empire. One day he sent a great army to attack one of these Greek cities, called Miletus. The people of Miletus fought bravely and the Athenians, their friends on the other side of the Aegean Sea, sent twenty ships to help.

But the little city of Miletus could not hold out for long against the huge army of King Darius. In the end the Persian soldiers stormed Miletus. The men were all killed, the women and children dragged away to become slaves, and the beautiful Greek city became a heap of smoking ruins. But the twenty Athenian ships escaped and King Darius was very angry that Athens, which was only a tiny speck compared with the Persian empire, had dared to resist him. It was such an insult and the king was so upset that he gave the order that at every meal he took, a servant had to call out: "King Darius, remember the Athenians." So he was already planning his revenge when the tyrant Hippias came to Persia. And Hippias promised King

Darius that if he were tyrant of Athens again, he would make the Athenians obedient servants of Persia.

But King Darius thought: "What is Athens? Just one city and I am king over hundreds of cities like Athens. If I send my army and my fleet I shall not be satisfied with Athens. I want the whole of Greece and a country which is divided into so many cities could never resist the power of my army. Yet perhaps I don't even have to send my army. I only have to threaten these Greeks with my power, and they will surrender." So the king sent messengers to every city in Greece demanding two things: water and earth. Water and earth were the tokens that they accepted King Darius as ruler over their land and sea.

Now there were some Greek cities such as Corinth, Thebes and Megara that were so afraid of the might of King Darius that they gave the messengers water and earth; the two tokens of surrender. But Sparta and Athens did not. The Spartans were not men of many words and they simply killed the messengers. That was their answer and King Darius could make of it what he liked. But the Athenians did something else. They threw one messenger into a river and said: "Here is your water," and they threw the other into a ditch and said: "Here is your earth." Then they let them return to their master.

When King Darius heard how Athens and Sparta had treated his messengers his fury was terrible. "I will show these miserable Greeks who is their lord and master. I will destroy the two cities, just as I destroyed Miletus. The proud Spartans will beg for mercy and the clever Athenians will bitterly regret their bit of fun with the messengers. The whole of Greece will tremble before the hordes of Persians that will sweep over the land like a hail storm," King Darius thought.

42. The Battle of Marathon

King Darius ordered his workmen to built a huge fleet to carry an army of a hundred thousand men across the Aegean Sea to Athens.

His shipbuilders laboured for a year, and when the ships were ready, the Persian soldiers went aboard. They were so certain of victory that they took great loads of iron chains to shackle the thousands of prisoners they imagined they would bring back as slaves. They also took large blocks of beautiful marble, so that they could put up a great monument to their victory. But King Darius stayed in Persia; such a vast army could not fail to win and there was no need for him to go with them.

Now Athens had only ten thousand men to fight the hundred thousand Persians: one Greek for every ten Persian warriors. But the Athenians hoped that Sparta would come to their aid. When the Persian army landed at a bay called Marathon, not far from Athens, the Athenians' fastest runner, a man called Phidippides, was sent to ask the Spartans for help. It was a journey of a hundred and fifty miles across mountains and rivers yet Phidippides made it in a day and a night.

The Spartans received Phidippides in a very friendly manner. They promised to come and help but, as they were celebrating a festival in honour of the Sun God, they could not come immediately. However, they told the runner, their soldiers would be there by the full moon in a week's time. So Phidippides ran back to Athens, again in one day and one night, bearing the Spartans' reply. This was grim news for Athens for the Persians had landed only twenty six miles away and would not wait a week to attack.

Many people in Athens thought there was now no hope and that their beloved city was already lost. But there was one man called Miltiades who gave them courage. He spoke to the Athenians in the Agora and said: "I have fought against the

Persians before and I know their ways. If we wait here in the city until they attack, then, most certainly, we will lose our city, our freedom, and our lives. But if we go to Marathon and attack the Persians, the goddess Pallas Athene will be with us and we may well win!" The people of Athens cheered and asked Miltiades to be their leader and general. Then they armed themselves and marched out to Marathon.

Now the Bay of Marathon where the Persians landed is surrounded by hills, and it was high on these hills that Miltiades and his Athenian soldiers made their camp. The Persians' great army was camped down on the shore close to the food and supplies in their ships. King Darius' warriors did not like the idea of attacking uphill: even though the Greeks were a much smaller force, they would have a great advantage. And so, for a couple of days, the two enemies, the little army of Athenians and the great army of the Persians, just looked at each other. Then Miltiades decided to wait no longer. He ordered his men to advance at a sharp run downhill and charge into the enemy. Once the Athenian soldiers started running they could not stop. Faster and faster they ran before crashing into the Persian army with tremendous force.

Under that terrific onslaught the Persians gave way. It was as if an avalanche had come down on them and they turned and ran towards the ships. But only some of these ships were lucky enough to escape; many had already been captured by the Athenians. And so the Persian army was utterly defeated. The Athenians had won the Battle of Marathon, a battle which is forever remembered in history. Then the rejoicing Athenians asked Phidippides, the runner, to sprint to Athens and take the news of their great victory.

Phidippides was already exhausted by the fighting and his three hundred-mile round trip to Sparta, but he immediately set out and ran the whole twenty six miles from Marathon to Athens without stopping. Breathless, he reached the Agora where people were anxiously waiting for news. "We have won!" he cried with the last of his strength. The next moment he fell down and died, having over-taxed his heart. Phidippides' heroic effort is remembered to this day and athletes from all over the world run twenty six miles in the Olympic Games in an event called the marathon. But our modern runners don't have to fight a battle before they run!

Of course Miltiades, who had led the Athenians to victory, was the hero of Athens. All fear of Persia was forgotten now the Greeks knew that the Persians could be beaten. A few days after the battle, the Spartan army arrived as promised. They were no longer needed but they honoured the Athenians and praised them for their victory.

Meanwhile Darius, the King of Persia, swore in his fury that he would not rest until he had taken revenge. He would send an army to Greece greater than any the world had ever seen before. But Darius died before the next invasion took place and it was his son who carried on the war against Greece.

43. Xerxes' Mighty Army

Darius had spent four years preparing an enormous army and fleet of ships to invade Greece when he died. His son, King Xerxes, spent another four years making the army and fleet even bigger. This time the plan was to attack Greece from both the land and the sea.

Now, in order to get to Greece by land the Persian army had to cross the narrow stretch of water called the Hellespont which runs between the Aegean Sea and the Black Sea. Using boats to ferry the army across would have taken too long so Xerxes ordered his engineers to build a huge bridge. But no sooner did the bridge span the strait than a great storm whipped the waves up so high that the bridge was smashed to bits. Xerxes was so furious that he had the engineers' heads cut off. But he also wanted to punish the waves that had dared to destroy the bridge built by the King of Kings. So the soldiers took whips and gave the sea a flogging for misbehaviour!

Soon other engineers built a new bridge, stronger than the first one. And when the immense army began to march across, it passed a great throne on which Xerxes sat. He wanted to see that army of his, the greatest army ever known. His soldiers were not only Persians — they came from every part of the empire. There were black warriors in leopard skins, Arabs on camels, Egyptians armed with battle axes, Babylonians in war chariots, horsemen from the Caucasus mountains as well as cooks and weapon-smiths and officers' servants. It was an incredibly large army of five million men, and it took seven days and seven nights for the whole horde to march over the bridge across the Hellespont. At the same time twelve hundred warships set off across the sea. It was as if the whole might of Asia was pouncing on the little country of Greece.

The Greeks had sent out some spies to discover how strong the Persians were, but they were captured and brought before

Xerxes. They expected to have their heads cut off but Xerxes smiled cunningly and said: "Let them see the strength, the majesty of Persia. Show them our army and then send them back to Greece. When the Greeks hear of our might they will lose all heart for fighting against us."

And it seemed that Xerxes was right. When his mighty army appeared in northern Greece, city after city opened its gates to the Persians. But in the south the cities of Athens and Sparta did not think of surrender. They were willing to fight and to die for their freedom.

Now, between the north and south of Greece there is a high mountain range. The only way to avoid the mountains is by travelling through the Pass of Thermopylae, a narrow strip of road between sheer cliffs and the sea. And the Persian army marched towards that pass. It was the Spartans who had the task of defending the Pass of Thermopylae and delaying the enemy as long as possible. However, the Olympics were being held and the Spartans would not have dreamt of missing the games for the sake of invading "barbarians". (The Greeks called all foreigners barbarians, which means people who are crude, ignorant and badly behaved.) So most of the Spartans went off calmly to watch the Olympic Games, leaving only a small band of Spartans to guard the pass.

You have read that the Persian army was five million strong. However, the Greeks who went to guard the pass numbered only five thousand, which is one Greek soldier for every thousand Persians. But the real heart and strength of the five thousand Greeks was the three hundred Spartans under their king whose name was Leonidas. And in the end it was really only the three hundred Spartans who dared to stand in the way of the immense Persian army.

44. Treachery at Thermopylae

As the Persian army approached the Pass of Thermopylae, their leader, Xerxes, learnt that the pass was defended by a small Greek force. But King Xerxes could not imagine that anyone would be mad enough to stand in the way. In fact, he expected that as soon as the Spartans saw his countless warriors, they would flee. But although the Spartans could see the vast hordes of approaching Persians, they had no intention of retreating.

King Xerxes was puzzled; he thought the Greeks must have taken leave of their senses. He sent a horseman to ride to the pass and report what he saw. The rider returned and said: "Some Spartans were wrestling and others practised jumping, but many were busy combing their long hair, as if they were preparing for a festival, not a battle." Xerxes was astonished, but then one of his generals said: "It is their custom, O King of Kings. When Spartan soldiers prepare themselves for battle they brush and comb their hair so they will look their best when they die. You can be sure, O King, that not one of these men will retreat."

But Xerxes laughed at the thought that such a little band of men would dare oppose him. He sent a messenger to Leonidas, the King of the Spartans, and the messenger said: "Xerxes, the King of Kings, will spare your life and the life of your men, if you hand over your swords and spears immediately." But Leonidas gave the messenger a short, truly Spartan answer: "Come and take them." This made the messenger angry and he shouted: "Do you know, there are so many of us that when we shoot our arrows they darken the sunlight?" And a Spartan soldier standing nearby smiled and said: "Good, we shall at least have some shade for the fighting."

Even when the messenger brought back the reply, Xerxes could still not believe the Spartans would fight. He waited four days for them to retreat but, on the fifth day, King Xerxes lost patience and gave his army the signal to attack.

Now the pass was only a narrow road flanked on one side by high cliffs and on the other by the sea. The Spartans stood shoulder to shoulder across the road so that their shields formed a wall. Time after time the Persians hurled themselves against the wall of shields but they could not break through. And every time they attacked many were struck down by the spears and swords of the Spartans. And, of course, because the road was so narrow, the five million Persians could not attack at the same time. And if too many Persians tried to get into the narrow pass, they only got in each other's way! But they fought on, and wave after wave of Persian warriors tried to break through the Spartan ranks. As soon as one Spartan was killed, the Spartan behind him took his place, so the unbroken wall of shields remained.

Soon there were such piles of dead Persians at the entrance to the pass that the bodies had to be cleared away before a new attack could be made. And still the wall of shields stood unbroken. Then King Xerxes sent in his best regiment, his bodyguard called The Immortals, to break through. Three times they stormed the Pass of Thermopylae, and three times they were driven back. By now King Xerxes was mad with fury. Many of his soldiers had lost heart and were no longer willing to continue the attack and die in that narrow passage. But the king ordered his officers to use whips and the Persian soldiers were driven into battle like animals. But, although many more Persians died, they could not break through.

After two days of fierce fighting, the wall of shields still stood unbroken. And Xerxes began to think that there was no hope of getting through. But that night a traitor, a Greek called Epialtes, came to King Xerxes and said: "I know a secret path over the hills. If your soldiers take that path they will come down into the Pass of Thermopylae behind the Spartans." King Xerxes gave Epialtes a large reward and during the night the traitor led the Persians along the secret path. When daylight came, the Spartans saw their enemies pouring down from the hills behind them. At the same time other Persian soldiers renewed their attack at the entrance to the pass. The Spartans knew that the battle was lost but they were determined to make the Persians pay dearly for the victory. They flung themselves at the barbarians like mad lions. When their spears broke they kept fighting with their short swords, and when the swords broke they fought with their bare hands until their last breath.

There was one Spartan who had been blinded in battle the day before. King Leonidas had sent him home with a servant but when the blind man, who was already some distance from the pass, heard the noise of battle, he made the servant take him back. "Which way are the Persians?" asked the blind man. The servant turned him in the direction of the enemy and the blind man drew his sword and flung himself into the fray to die fighting with his comrades.

So Leonidas and his fearless men all died. But their brave stand against the great army of Xerxes was never forgotten. The Battle of Thermopylae was the pride of all Greece. Many years later, the Spartans placed a stone lion in the Pass of Thermopylae in honour of King Leonidas. Under it the inscription reads:

Go, tell the Spartans, thou that passest by
That here obedient to their laws we lie.

45. Ships of War

In spite of their heroic stand, the Spartans had not been able to stop the Persian army marching south through the Pass of Thermopylae. And so Athens once again held the fate of Greece in its hands.

You have already heard about a great hero of Athens called Miltiades. After leading the Athenians to victory at Marathon, Miltiades had died after being wounded in a sea battle and it was left to another man with foresight and courage to help the Athenians in their hour of need. His name was Themistocles. Even when he was young Themistocles was different from other boys. While other children played games, Themistocles stayed in his room and made up long speeches. Imagining that one of his friends was accused of a crime, he would make up a speech to defend him. And, unlike most Athenians, Themistocles did not care for art and beauty. When he was given a lyre, he said: "I don't care for music. There is only one art that interests me and that is the art of making a country powerful and great!"

Now, when Darius was still King of Persia and his army was defeated by the Athenians at Marathon, the people of Athens thought the Persians would never threaten them again. But Themistocles believed that the Persians would definitely return, and he used all his eloquence to convince the Athenians that they should spend money building warships. The people of Athens did not know what to do so they sent messengers to the Oracle of Delphi for advice. And the Oracle gave the strange reply: "Only wooden walls can save Athens."

The Athenians were puzzled by this answer, but Themistocles said: "The wooden walls mean nothing other than ships — warships. Listen to me, people of Athens. We cannot beat the Persians on land but if we beat their fleet, if we beat them at sea, we shall win the war." So, in the end, the Athenians built a fleet of three hundred warships. And that fleet, along with another hundred Spartan ships, was all the Greeks had to fight the mighty army and twelve hundred ships of King Xerxes.

The Persians marched south towards Athens unopposed. No Athenian army came to meet them. Under the command of Themistocles, all the Athenian warriors had manned their ships while the women, children and old people were taken by boat to the nearby island of Salamis. So when the Persians arrived in the city of Athens they found it deserted. Immediately they set fire to the buildings and, from the island of Salamis, the Athenians saw their beloved city go up in flames. But they also saw in the Bay of Salamis their only hope; the wooden walls of the Athenian fleet. And they saw something else; the Persian fleet of 1200 ships was approaching and it seemed as if the whole sea was covered with warships. Now, the Spartans were fearless fighters on land but they did not feel so confident as sailors and when they saw the vast Persian fleet they lost heart and decided to sail away.

But when Themistocles heard what was going on, he played a cunning trick on the Spartans. He sent a servant to King Xerxes with the message: "My master, Themistocles, is really your friend and he hopes that when you have conquered Greece, you will reward him for his advice. And my master's advice is to order your fleet to block the Bay of Salamis so that not one Greek ship can escape. Then you can catch the whole lot like rats in a trap." Xerxes was very pleased with this advice. His ships blocked the bay where the tiny Greek fleet waited and the Spartans had to stay and fight whether they liked it or not. But as soon as the Persians closed in, Themistocles gave the order to attack, and when the Spartans saw how bravely the Athenians fought, they took heart and joined the battle.

Now the Greek boats were much smaller than the big, heavy, Persian ships. But being small they were much more agile and could dart in and out of the Persian battle lines. Their main armament was a long ram mounted on the front of the boat on the water line. And so the little Greek warships twisted and turned until they were in a position to ram the Persian ships in the side, smashing the enemy's planking so that the sea poured in through gaping holes and the boat sank. Some of the lumbering Persian ships ran into each other or hit cliffs as they tried to manoeuvre in the narrow bay. Soon the sea was full of sinking ships, broken oars, shattered planks and drowning sailors. Some of the Persian ships were rowed by Greek slaves and in the heat of battle the slaves overpowered their Persian masters and joined the Greek fleet. At this, the remaining Persian ships turned and fled. So the Battle of Salamis was a complete victory for the Athenians.

King Xerxes had watched the battle from a high throne on the shore. When he saw his great fleet smashed he was filled with fear and despair. He rode away with his bodyguard and, without stopping to rest, travelled all the way to the Hellespont and on to Persia. His pride had been humbled and his boasting shown to be hollow.

Xerxes' army also turned back. But the Persian ships that carried the supplies of food had gone and the soldiers were starving. Disease broke out and thousands died. Yet for a whole year the retreating Persians continued to ravage parts of Greece, but they were no longer the proud army they had been. Then the Spartans took the opportunity to revenge King Leonidas and in the great Battle of Plataea they killed thousands of Persian warriors. Only a few thousand barbarians escaped to return home. Never again did any of the Persian kings try to invade Greece for they had learned a terrible lesson.

All the Greek cities recognized that it was Themistocles who had saved them from defeat. His idea to build a fleet of warships had been the right one. The Spartans presented him with a beautiful golden chariot but the greatest honour was given to him at the Olympic Games. When Themistocles arrived to take his seat, hundreds of thousands of people from every city in Greece stood up and cheered. When the cheering died down everyone expected Themistocles to make a long speech, but the great Athenian, who was famous for his eloquence, spoke as few words as a Spartan. He said: "Friends, this is the happiest day of my life."

46. The Judgment
of the Shards

The Athenians and the Spartans had saved Greece by defeating the mighty Xerxes. But what would have happened if the Persians had conquered Greece!

Now, we go to school to learn from our teachers. And, of course, when our teachers were young they were taught by their teachers and, in turn, those teachers were taught by their teachers. And so we can go back further and further until we come to a time long ago when people could not have taught children any of the things you learn now. Those people, long, long ago, could neither read nor write. In the case of Britain it was the Romans who came and taught the primitive people. Not only did they teach reading and writing, but also how to build houses, roads and temples.

But, at one time the Romans were also a primitive people. And as the Romans taught the Britons, so the Greeks taught the Romans. All the knowledge that the Romans went on to teach the ancient Britons came from the Greeks. The people of Greece were the first civilized people of Europe. They were the first people in Europe to study nature and discover the secrets of science. They were the first people in Europe to build beautiful cities and create great works of art. And they were the first to love knowledge and art. And all these things — their knowledge of art, architecture, science and philosophy — the Greeks taught to other nations.

Now, as we have seen, the people of Athens were not only brave and clever but also loved beauty. However, some people might say that they did have faults: one great failing was that they were not very reliable. They would, for instance, honour a person for some great deed, but a few years or even a month later, they would turn against him. The Athenians changed their minds often and if they did not like one of their leaders, they banished him from Athens and he had to leave the city.

But how did the people of Athens decide if they liked a man or not? It was done in this way: in a corner of the Agora there was a heap of broken pottery or shards. Every year in March the people gathered in the Agora and wrote on a shard the name of the Athenian they disliked most. At the end of the day the archons counted the shards and the person whose name was written most often had to leave the city for ten years. This was called ostracism or the judgment of the shards.

Now Themistocles was, as we have seen, clever and brave. But he was also greedy and ambitious. At one time, long before the Battle of Salamis, he had been a judge in Athens. But he was not a fair judge: if you wanted to win in a court case you only had to give him money and he would see to it that you won. Or, if you were Themistocles' friend, you could be sure you would win your case. Now there was one man in Athens, Aristides, who was absolutely fair. The people called him Aristides the Just. He had been a general in the Persian wars and had fought bravely with Miltiades at Marathon. He was also a judge, but for Aristides neither money nor friendship made any difference: if you were right you won, and if you were in the wrong you lost.

As you can imagine, Aristides and Themistocles did not like each other. In fact Aristides warned the Athenians that Themistocles was not honest. He said Themistocles took bribes. Aristides even suggested that the Athenians should not listen to Themistocles' advice to build a fleet of warships but should fight the Persians on land instead. But Themistocles answered: "Let us have the judgment of the shards. Let us see which one of us should leave Athens!" So the people of Athens went to the Agora to write on the shards.

As Aristides stood in the Agora a peasant came up to him. The peasant, who did not know who Aristides was, said: "Would you help me please? I cannot write so can you put the name of Aristides on this shard for me?"

Then Aristides asked: "What have you got against this man?" "Oh," said the peasant, "I am annoyed that everyone calls him The Just."

The honest Aristides wrote his own name down and gave the peasant the shard. And in the judgment of the shards Aristides was ostracized and had to leave Athens.

But Aristides was allowed to return just before the Battle of Salamis, and he fought bravely alongside Themistocles against the Persians. Now, the Greeks had found a lot of treasure on the captured Persian ships and everyone who had taken part in the battle was promised a share. But Aristides refused his share and remained poor.

After the war, Aristides again warned the Athenians that Themistocles was not honest. At first no one listened to him. But the day came when, urged on by Aristides, the Athenians finally wrote the name of Themistocles — hero of Salamis but greedy, dishonest judge — on their shards. So Themistocles had to leave Athens.

He was so bitter at the way the Athenians had treated him that he went to the arch-enemy of Greece, the Persian king Artaxerxes, Xerxes' son. Strangely enough, the king received Themistocles kindly and said: "I have offered a great prize to the man who would deliver Themistocles to me. Now you have delivered yourself to me so the prize is yours." And so the hero who had saved Athens and Greece spent the last years of his life in Persia. But the Athenians did honour Aristides who, although perhaps not as clever as Themistocles, was honest, fair and just. So it happened that Themistocles died in Persia, forgotten by his city, but when Aristides died, three years later, the whole of Athens, rich and poor, mourned him.

47. The Golden Age

Miltiades, Leonidas and Themistocles were the Greek leaders who were great in war. It is, however, much more difficult to be a leader and ruler in times of peace. But after the Persian wars Athens was lucky enough to have a great leader called Pericles. And it was this man who brought to Athens what is known as the Golden Age.

Although Pericles had fought bravely in the Persian wars, his aim was to make the city of Athens great in peace time. He had all the qualities of a great statesman of those days: he came from a noble family; he loved all the arts, he was generous and he was absolutely fair and honest. And, like a true Athenian, he could speak wisely and beautifully, moving the hearts of all who heard him.

The tall, handsome Pericles became an archon, but his fine qualities shone out and, in the end, the other archons recognized him as the true leader. So for many years Pericles was the ruler of Athens. But he never misused his power or tried to make himself richer. Nor did he ever try to harm anyone for his only aim in life was to make Athens great in works of peace.

But keeping the peace was no easy task. As soon as the Persian wars were over, the other Greek city states, especially Sparta, became envious of Athens. Only Pericles' wisdom and eloquence prevented this jealousy from leading to war, and for fifty years the cities of Greece lived in peace.

Pericles also kept the peace between rich and poor in Athens. He made a law that prevented any Athenian from going hungry. The taxes the rich paid helped to provide food for people who had no money to buy it. He also ruled that every Athenian, rich or poor, could attend an enormous open air theatre and watch plays free of charge. The theatre, which could seat thousands, was built near the Temple of Pallas Athene at the base of the Acropolis. It was, in fact, during the time that Pericles was the ruler of Athens that the temple was built and the sculptor Phidias made, from ivory and gold, a magnificent statue of the goddess.

Phidias and Pericles were great friends, and, at this time in Athens, there were other great men whose names are still remembered. Such a man was Hippocrates. After medical students pass their exams but before the can become doctors they must swear an oath. The students must promise that they will use their knowledge only to help and to cure because many medicines can also be deadly poisons. This promise is called the Hippocratic oath, after the great doctor Hippocrates who lived in Athens at the time of Pericles.

We heard how Pericles made a law allowing rich and poor alike to go to the theatre for free. This huge open air theatre was the first in the world. And Athenians like Aeschylus and Euripides who wrote the plays, both tragedies and comedies, were the first playwrights. Even today, the plays these great men wrote are still performed.

It was also during Pericles' time that men began to study the secrets of nature. These men who used their thinking to understand the world were called philosophers and one of the finest philosophers the world has ever known lived in Athens at the time of Pericles. His name was Socrates.

Now the very first man to write a book about history also lived in Athens when Pericles was the ruler. He was called Herodotus and he is known as the father of history because no one had thought of writing history down before.

All these great men — doctors, scientists, playwrights, historians and philosophers — were Pericles' friends. And Athens itself flourished: through trade it became the richest city in Greece; through its great artists it became the most beautiful city in Greece; and through its philosophers and writers it became the most famous city in Greece.

The Golden Age of Athens lasted for fifty years and by that time Pericles was an old man. By then the Spartans had become so jealous of Athens' fame and power that war broke out. Soon after, Athens was struck by an epidemic. The black plague killed thousands, including the great statesman Pericles. Yet the whole of mankind has benefited from that fifty years of peace and progress in Athens.

48. The Love of Wisdom

Greece, then, became the country from which all other nations learned. Even now, nearly all the words used in science: such as astronomy, which means the science of the stars; biology, the science of living things; physics, the science of the forces in nature, are Greek words. The Greeks also recognized that the art of thinking in the right way was a science. They called it philosophy which means love of wisdom. And you remember that one of the world's first philosophers was a man called Socrates.

Now, just imagine you had come to Athens after the Persian wars. The Athenians were busy rebuilding their city and making it even more beautiful than it was before. So, you arrive at the harbour where hundreds of ships with sails of all colours load great urns of olive oil, works of art and goatskins filled with wine. From the deep blue sea you turn landwards. Behind the houses of Athens stands the Acropolis with its many marble temples. The highest building is the Temple of Pallas Athene, the Parthenon, with its statue of the goddess made by the sculptor Phidias.

Now you walk from the harbour to the city. The houses are only one storey high and they are built round a central courtyard. There is no pavement to walk on and the narrow streets bustle with pedestrians, horsemen and donkeys laden with food or other goods. Along the sides of the streets are many statues of gods and heroes and famous men like Miltiades, Aristides, and Themistocles. In the distance is the great open air theatre with its stone seats rising in tiers in a semi-circle around the stage. The performances are all free, and when there are festivals several plays are performed. It takes a whole day to watch them all and then the audience decides which was the best. The actors wear masks and some walk on stilts under their long robes, so that they look bigger.

You walk on through the streets and all around you are

beautifully dressed Greeks. Over a tunic they wear something like a big sheet which is draped in many folds over the left shoulder. Now you come to the Agora. Nearby there are food stalls and people buying, selling and talking. In the square itself you notice a group of young men listening intently and eagerly to an older man. He is not handsome like most of the other Athenians; he has a rather flat, wide nose and a long unkempt beard. His robe is made of rough cloth and there are no sandals on his feet. Yet the handsome young men, many of them from rich and noble families, stand as if spellbound around the bearded barefooted man whose name is Socrates. And the young men stand listening so intently because the great teacher of thinking never wrote his wisdom down. Instead he taught his pupils by conversation.

Socrates came from a poor family. Later in life he could easily have acquired wealth, yet money and luxuries meant nothing to him. He said: "The less you need, the happier you are," and his only aim in life was to become wise. Once the king of another country invited Socrates to come to his court and offered him great honours and wealth. Socrates answered: "Here in Athens a loaf of bread costs only a few coppers, clear water costs nothing at all. And that's all I need. I am sorry but you have nothing to offer that I want." The rich young men who listened to Socrates would often invite him to their banquets and feasts; he would come but eat only a little.

By nature, Socrates had a wild temper. But he trained himself until nothing could make him angry. One day he had an argument with a rude, mean fellow, and the man got so wild that he struck Socrates in the face. But Socrates said calmly: "What a pity I did not know this morning that I would need a helmet."

Yet, Socrates was one of the bravest men in Athens, and he took part in several battles. Once, when a friend was badly wounded, Socrates covered the soldier with his own shield to protect him and, standing over him, fought off the enemy. The Athenians wanted to reward him for his courage but Socrates refused and insisted that the reward was given to his wounded friend.

Now, Socrates made his pupils think for themselves. One of

his pupils, a young man, was very nervous about making a speech before the people of Athens. So Socrates asked: "Tell me, would you be afraid to speak before a carpenter?"

"No," said the young man.

"But," said Socrates, "a grocer would frighten you?"

"No, he would not," the young man answered.

"Would you be scared of a sailor?"

"No," cried the young man.

"Well," said Socrates, "if you are not afraid of each one by himself, why should you be nervous and afraid of them when they are together?" And the next day the young man made a wonderful speech, and was not nervous at all.

Once an Athenian asked the Oracle of Delphi: "Who is the wisest man of Greece?" And the Oracle answered: "Socrates."

But when Socrates was told this, he said: "I will tell you why the Oracle said I am wise. Other people say they know this or they know that, and think they are clever. But I know only one thing: that I know nothing! That's all my wisdom."

So you see, he was a humble and modest man. But the richest, cleverest young men of Athens honoured, respected and loved him. Yet, even this wise and humble man had enemies.

49. Alcibiades the Traitor

In ancient Persia it was the god Ahura Mazda who came to King Djemshid in a dream and gave him the idea of making a plough. In Babylon it was Ea, the God of the Dawn, who told the Babylonians how to make bricks. And in ancient Egypt it was the god Osiris who taught the Egyptians to write hieroglyphics.

In those ancient times, wisdom came in dreams from the gods, and the thoughts and ideas that came to people were a gift from the gods. But in ancient Greece, for the first time, human beings learnt to *think* for themselves. And Socrates was one of the greatest teachers of the art of thinking. Geometry, physics and algebra were all developed in Greece after Socrates taught people how to think.

However, when Socrates was teaching his pupils all this wonderful knowledge, life in Greece was not easy. After the Spartans and Athenians saved Greece from the barbarians, during the time of Pericles, there was fifty years of peace. But then a long and terrible war broke out between Sparta and Athens. Other Greek cities joined in, sometimes on one side, sometimes on the other, and the whole country was plunged into battle and strife.

The people of Athens fought as bravely as the Spartans, and even won some battles. But you have heard how the Athenians had one weakness: they would praise a man one day and turn against him the next. It was the same with their generals. They would honour a general if he won a battle but shout for his death if he lost, even if it was not his fault. The generals too, changed sides, fighting first for Athens and then against it. One such man was called Alcibiades.

Now Alcibiades, a pupil of Socrates, was the most handsome and richest young man in Athens. He was generous, full of wit and fun, and very popular. But he was also thoroughly spoilt. One day he walked into the Athenian Council where grave and serious matters of war were being discussed. He had hidden some birds under his robe, and when he suddenly set them free the whole council was in uproar. Anybody else would have been punished but not Alcibiades, the favourite of Athens.

Another time he bought a very expensive dog with a long bushy tail. All the Athenians admired it but the very next day Alcibiades cut the dog's tail off. When his friends told Alcibiades that the people of Athens were angry and upset by his deed, he answered: "As long as they talk about me, I don't mind whether they say good things or bad things."

So you see, he wanted to draw attention to himself, and did not care who he hurt or upset. But there was one man who could make Alcibiades feel ashamed, and that was Socrates. Alcibiades loved Socrates and he had good reason to for he was the wounded man Socrates saved in battle.

Now, Alcibiades was very ambitious and wanted to show the Athenians that he was a great leader in war. One day a huge fleet set sail from Athens with Alcibiades as one of the commanders. But the night before the fleet set out something happened which shocked the Athenians: every statue of the god Hermes in the city was mysteriously damaged. Each and every statue had an arm or a nose broken, or its ears knocked off. Now this was something terrible for the Athenians, something which could only be punished by death. The people of Athens decided that only Alcibiades would do such a thing and, although the fleet had sailed, they sent out two ships to bring the culprit back.

Alcibiades denied that he had anything to do with such a stupid prank, but he did not go back to Athens to defend himself. Instead he fled to Sparta, the enemy of Athens. There, Alcibiades, who had lived in luxury in Athens, shared the harsh, simple life of the Spartans. But his pride and conceit soon turned people against him and again he fled. This time he went to the Persians — the arch-enemies of all Greeks. He even persuaded the Persians to help Sparta in the war against Athens.

You can imagine how bitterly the Athenians now hated Alcibiades who had become a traitor, an enemy of his own city. But their hatred also turned against Socrates, Alcibiades' teacher and friend. They said Socrates had given young men all kinds of wrong ideas. They said he was a bad influence. They said Socrates should die so that he could no longer poison the minds of the young.

So it happened that Socrates, the wisest of the Athenians, was brought before a court and condemned to death. Socrates' pupils stood faithfully by him; they even bribed the jailors to let their teacher escape. But Socrates refused the offer for he would not disobey the law of Athens.

In Athens a condemned man was not hanged or beheaded. Instead he was given a cup of the poisonous plant hemlock to drink. And that is how the philosopher Socrates met his death.

50. The Death of Socrates

Socrates' pupil Plato, who also became a great philosopher, wrote an account of the last day of Socrates' life in prison in a book called Phaedo.

This is what he wrote:

The jailer entered and said: "To you, Socrates, whom I know to be the noblest, gentlest and best of all who ever came to this place, I will not inspire the angry feelings of others who rage and swear at me when, in obedience of the authorities, I bid them drink the poison. Indeed I am sure you will not be angry with me. And so farewell, and try to bear lightly what must needs be; you know my errand." Then brushing back tears he turned away and went out.

Socrates said: "I return your good wishes and will do as you bid." Then turning to us he said: "How kind this man is. Since I have been in prison he was as good to me as could be."

The jailer returned carrying the cup of poison. Socrates said: "You, my good friend, who have experience in this matter, shall give me directions how I am to proceed." The man answered: "When you have drunk the poison you have only to walk about until your legs are heavy and then to lie down and the poison will act." At the same time he handed the cup to Socrates who, in the easiest and gentlest manner, without the least fear, without any change in his face or colour, took the cup and raising it to his lips, readily and cheerfully, drank the poison. Up to this moment most of us had been able to control our sorrow; but now when we saw him drinking and that he had finished the draught, we could no longer forbear; and in spite of myself, my own tears were flowing fast. I wept not for him but at the thought of my own loss in having to part from such a friend. At that moment Apollodorus broke out in a loud cry which made us all weep openly and bitterly.

Socrates alone remained calm. "What is this strange outcry?" he said. "Earlier this day I have sent away the women (his wife and sisters) in order that they should not behave here in this way. Be quiet then and have patience." When we heard his words we were ashamed and held back our tears. And he walked about until his legs began to fail. The he lay down on his back as he had been told. The jailer who had given him the poison, after a while, pressed the foot of Socrates and asked if he could feel it — and he answered: "No."

Then the man pressed his leg and thigh and thus going higher he showed us that he was growing cold and stiff. Then Socrates touched his own body and said: "When the poison reaches the heart, that will be the end."

Then Socrates covered his face with a cloth but once more he uncovered it and said to one of his friends: "Crito, I made a promise to sacrifice a cock to the god Asclepius [the God of Healing]. Will you remember to pay this debt for me?" "I will," said Crito, "is there anything else you want?"

There was no answer. A moment or two later there was a slight movement. The jailer covered Socrates, and Crito closed his eyes.

Such was the end of our friend, of whom I may truly say that of all the men of this time whom I have known, he was the wisest, the most fair-minded, and the best.★

So that was the brave way that Socrates died. But what had happened to Alcibiades, whose behaviour had made the Athenians turn against Socrates? You have heard how he fled first to Sparta and then to the Greeks' old enemies, the Persians. He even persuaded the Persian king to help Sparta, and Persian mercenaries — Egyptians, Africans, even Greeks — were sent to Greece to help Sparta in the war against Athens. The Athenians were no match for the Spartans' strengthened army and lost battle after battle. They had no great leader like Miltiades, who had led them in the Battle of Marathon, or Themistocles, who beat the Persian fleet at the Bay of Salamis. In despair they sent a messenger to Alcibiades asking him to come back and lead them in the war against Sparta.

Alcibiades returned to Athens and was welcomed by the same people who had wanted to put him on trial for damaging the statues of the god Hermes. Then he led the Athenian army

★ Retold from Plato's *Phaedo*.

out to defeat the Spartans in a great battle. From that day on the Spartans hated him and swore to take revenge. In the meantime Alcibiades was honoured, praised, and cheered by the Athenians. He was given command of the Athenian fleet in the Aegean Sea. But one day the fleet was attacked by the combined Spartan and Persian fleet. Alcibiades was not with his ship for he was enjoying himself with some friends in Athens. Without its great leader the Athenian fleet was defeated and many ships sunk.

Once more the Athenians turned on Alcibiades. They blamed him for the defeat and drove him out of the city. Now Alcibiades had no friends anywhere. Athens, Sparta, Persia; he had let everyone down, he had betrayed them all. Surprisingly, the Persians allowed him to flee to their territory, but they no longer trusted him. The Spartans had not forgiven him and they send a man to murder Alcibiades. The Persian king knew about it but he did nothing to protect or warn Alcibiades and he was killed by the assassin's dagger. So died the most handsome and richest son of Athens; a pupil of Socrates.

After Alcibiades, Athens had no clever general to lead them into battle. In the fighting that followed the Spartans destroyed the last of the Athenians' great fleet of warships and attacked the city of Athens itself. In the end Athens surrendered to the Spartans and the defensive walls of the city were torn down so that the Athenians would not be able to go to war again.

The whole of Greece suffered in the fighting, known as the Peloponnesian War, which dragged on for almost thirty years.

Alexander the Great

51. Taming Bucephalus

The Greeks had built a number of cities on the coast across the Aegean Sea. One of them, called Ephesus, was famous for a wonderful temple dedicated to Diana, the Goddess of Hunting. For hundreds of years people came from far and near to admire the building and its many statues.

Now, in Ephesus there was a man called Herostratus who wanted to be famous. He wanted his name to be remembered forever. But he was not clever nor was he a great warrior or philosopher. One day he had the mad idea that he could make himself famous if he destroyed the temple. So one night he set fire to the building and it went up in flames. Of course, he was condemned to death and executed. But he had achieved his mad ambition; everyone in Greece knew his name and cursed his evil deed.

Now the very same night as the temple was destroyed, a baby boy was born who was to become not only truly famous for great deeds but also one of the greatest kings who ever lived. And this child was born in a country to the north of Greece called Macedonia.

Macedonia was a small country of no importance but, in time, it came to be important, and it happened like this: In the war between Athens and Sparta which dragged on for so long, Alcibiades, who deserted the Athenians and joined first the Spartans, then the Persians, and yet again changed sides to help the Athenians, was in the end killed by the Spartans. Yet still the war went on, until, after twenty-seven years of fighting, the Athenians were exhausted and surrendered to the Spartans.

The Spartans could have destroyed Athens and made the Athenians their slaves, but they remembered that the once great city had saved Greece from the Persians. So the Spartans let the Athenians live and carry on as before only they could not rule themselves; they had to obey the kings of Sparta.

All the cities of Greece had suffered in the long years of war and thousands of lives had been lost. Even Sparta was weakened. But Macedonia, a tiny country of wild, rugged mountains, little towns, and rough peasants and shepherds, had not taken part in the war. Now, when the King of Macedonia saw how the Greek cities had been weakened, he thought it was a good time to make himself the master of the whole of Greece.

The king's name was Philip and he led his sturdy men down from the mountains to conquer the Greek cities. Of course they fought against him, but in vain. Not even the united forces of Sparta and Athens could stand against the Macedonians, and in one great battle, at Cheroneia, both the Spartan and Athenian armies were defeated. And so Philip, the king of tiny Macedonia, achieved what no Persian king had managed: he became king and master of the whole of Greece.

Now, the child born in the night the Temple of Diana at Ephesus was destroyed was the King of Macedonia's son. And the soothsayers, the priests who could foretell the future, said that this child would become a famous ruler. The boy was called Alexander and, because he did go on to achieve great things, he is known in history books as Alexander the Great.

Even in his youth Alexander showed that he was destined for greatness. One day, when he was about fourteen years old, a merchant offered his father a beautiful black horse, called Bucephalus. First King Philip, and then his best horsemen tried to mount Bucephalus. But the horse reared and kicked, and no one could get into the saddle. In the end the king got very angry and told the merchant to take the useless beast away. But, young Alexander, who had been watching, asked his father to let him try. At first his father refused; he did not want his son to get hurt. But Alexander insisted and Philip eventually gave him permission.

But, you see, Alexander had noticed that what was frightening the horse was its own shadow which it could see on the ground. The prince approached Bucephalus, spoke quietly to it, then took the reins and turned the horse round. Now it faced the sun so its shadow fell behind it. Then Alexander leapt into the saddle and, as the horse was no longer frightened, it obeyed him as if it were tame. The prince rode Bucephalus — which means Bull's Head — up and down the field, then dismounted. King Philip felt very proud of his son and said: "The horse is yours, Alexander. But I think you should look for a larger kingdom; my own will be too small for you."

Alexander was not only a good horseman, he also excelled in using weapons. And he was so good at gymnastics that his teachers said he should compete in the Olympic Games. But Alexander answered: "Yes, I would, but only if the other competitors are also kings!" So, you see, he was proud and he remained so all his life.

Yet there was one person whom the prince loved and respected and that was his teacher, Aristotle. You remember Socrates, and his pupil, Plato. Now Aristotle, who was one of the wisest men in Greece, was one of Plato's pupils. And Alexander was so grateful for the wisdom and the art of thinking that he learnt from Aristotle that he once said: "You are more than my father to me. My father can only give me things of this earth, but you have awakened my spirit."

Of all the books, Alexander loved best the poems of Homer, which tell about the Trojan War and the adventures of Odysseus. Every night, before he went to sleep, he put the book under his pillow so that he could read it first thing in the morning.

52. Dreams of Conquest

When Alexander was still a young boy, he heard his father's courtiers speak about a battle King Philip had won. Suddenly Alexander broke into tears, and, surprised, the courtiers asked: "What is the matter? Why are you crying?" And Alexander replied: "If my father goes on like that, gaining victory after victory, there will be nothing left for me to conquer when I am grown up!"

But Alexander's turn came sooner than he expected. Philip had become master of Greece after defeating the combined forces of Sparta and Athens in the Battle of Cheroneia. The king was full of plans for even greater conquests but, only two years after that battle, he was murdered and Alexander became king.

He was then only twenty years old. And the cities of Greece, which had never liked the idea of being ruled by Macedonia, thought it would be easy to regain their freedom now that they had only a young man to deal with. With great contempt they called Alexander "that boy" and rose in rebellion against him.

However, by that time, the Athenians had become well-to-do businessmen, who cared little for glory or freedom. They were really too well fed and lazy to go and fight although they still admired eloquence and beautiful speaking. And there were men in Athens who had so perfected the art of speaking that people would come and listen to their speeches for the sheer pleasure of it. And the most famous of these orators was Demosthenes.

But at first Demosthenes was not a good speaker at all. He had a slight stammer, his voice was weak, and when he spoke everything he said was in the same tone of voice. When he stood up on the rostrum in the Agora and made his first stammering speech in a voice so weak that it could hardly be heard the Athenians just laughed and walked away.

But Demosthenes was not dismayed; he was determined to

become a great orator. Whenever there was a storm he went down to the sea and practised his speeches until he could shout loudly enough to be heard above the roaring wind and waves. He put pebbles into his mouth and forced himself to speak clearly in spite of having a mouth full of stones. Then he locked himself in his house and practised changing his tone of voice. And Demosthenes was so determined to succeed that he shaved one side of his head so that he would be ashamed to leave the house before he had become a skilful orator.

And when, after a year of hard training, he went to the Agora to speak, the Athenians were held by his speech as if by a spell. Never before had there been such a great orator. Yet Demosthenes did not just speak for the sake of it; he wanted the Athenians to be as brave as they had been when Miltiades and Themistocles were alive. He wanted them to rise and fight the Macedonians as they had once fought against the Persians. And so eloquent and powerful were Demosthenes' speeches that the Athenians eventually joined the other Greek cities in rebellion against Alexander.

But Demosthenes did not know that this Macedonian "boy" was an even greater general than his father. After Alexander conquered one of the rebellious cities, called Thebes, and burnt it, the other cities quickly changed their minds. With great haste they sent messengers to Alexander to assure him they were his obedient and loyal subjects. At first Alexander wanted to execute Demosthenes, but in the end he spared the great orator's life.

Now Alexander really wanted to be friends with the Greeks. He wanted them to support him wholeheartedly because he had great plans. But to accomplish these plans he needed help so he called the leaders of every Greek city to a meeting. They met in Corinth and Alexander spoke to them and said: "You have all heard of the Persian wars. You have heard how your forefathers fought bravely at Marathon, Thermopylae, Salamis and Plataea and, in the end, drove the Persians out. But this is not enough. What I plan to do is conquer Persia. Once the Persians invaded us, but now we shall go to their country and fight. And we shall win, just as once, in the old days, we won here in Greece."

And the leaders of the Greek states cheered Alexander and

hailed him as the king and commander-in-chief of all Greeks. Only the Spartans grumbled. They said: "We Spartans only fight under a Spartan leader. You can destroy our city, you can kill us all but we will not fight for you." But Alexander answered: "You can stay at home, I will conquer Persia without you!" And all the other Greeks cheered him again, happy at the thought that the time had come when Greek armies would march into Persia.

But the Spartans were not the only ones to be unimpressed by Alexander. Living in Corinth was a rather strange man called Diogenes who tried to live up to Socrates' ideal that the less you need, the happier you are. But Diogenes went much further than Socrates. Instead of living in a house he slept in an old, empty barrel. He had also thrown away his cup when he discovered that he could drink just as well by scooping water into the hollow of his hands.

Now, Alexander had heard about this man so he decided to go and see him. He found Diogenes, who had long unkempt hair and a beard, and was dressed in rags, sitting outside his barrel in the sun. And Alexander asked him: "Is there any favour I can do for you? Ask me for anything you like and it will be given to you." "Yes," said Diogenes. "You just happen to be standing between me and the sun. Step aside a little so that I can sun myself." The courtiers who were with Alexander were outraged that an old man in rags dared to speak in such a way to their king. But Alexander said to them: "You know, if I were not Alexander, I should like to be Diogenes."

But Alexander, being himself, could never be satisfied with a barrel. He was not satisfied with Macedonia nor even the whole of Greece; for him it had to be an empire such as the world had never seen.

53. The Gordian Knot

Now Alexander the Great did not want to conquer Persia just for the sake of gaining more power. He had, in fact, a rather different reason. From his tutor, Aristotle, he had learnt about ancient Atlantis being swallowed by the sea and the new beginning that mankind made in India. He had also learnt about the old wisdom of the Persian, Babylonian and Egyptian civilizations. But now Greece had brought a new wisdom into the world; the art of thinking. And Alexander wanted the ancient wisdom of Asia and the new wisdom of Greece to be united. However, the only way he could see of bringing the knowledge of Asia and Europe together was by making all these countries into one great empire. He did not want to go to war to destroy towns and cities or to make the Persians slaves. Instead he hoped to create something new; an empire where the knowledge of Asia and Europe could become one.

Alexander was only twenty three years old when his army of thirty thousand Macedonians and Greeks set out to conquer the mighty Persians. The Persians did not think that such a force would be much of a threat, so Alexander's army marched through northern Greece and crossed the Hellespont without opposition. But when they came to a river called the Granicus they saw an immense Persian army waiting on the other side. Fearlessly Alexander rode Bucephalus into the water and his faithful Macedonian and Greek horseman followed. But there was a strong current and as the horses struggled desperately to keep their footing, the Persians sent a hail of arrows from the bank.

But, spurred on by the courage of their young king, the Greeks gained the far bank and a ferocious battle began. Two Persian officers recognized Alexander by the white plumes on his helmet, his shining armour and his black horse, and immediately attacked him. One rose in his stirrups and brought his battle-axe down on Alexander's helmet. The helmet split in two, and the other Persian lifted his axe for the death blow. But a brave Macedonian called Clitus saw the danger and killed the Persian with his sword while Alexander struck the other down.

So fiercely did the Macedonians fight that the Persians eventually turned and fled, leaving thousands of dead and wounded behind. But the Greeks had lost only a very few men and the battle at the Granicus was their first great victory. And from that day the brave Clitus, who had saved Alexander's life, was invited to sit next to the king at meal times; something that was regarded as a great honour.

After the Battle of Granicus the Greeks arrived in the city of Gordium. In the Temple of Zeus there was an ox-cart which had belonged to a peasant who had been chosen to be King of Gordium many, many years before. The yoke of the cart was tied to the pole with a very complicated knot. So skilfully had it been tied that no matter how you tried to trace its twists and turns, you could never find where the knot began or ended. It was known as the Gordian Knot, and there was a prophecy that whoever could untie it would became the master of Asia.

Alexander went to the temple and the priests showed him the knot which no one could untie. The king looked at the twisted strands, then he said: "There is only one way to deal with this knot." He drew his sword and, with one stroke, cut right through it. So Alexander had undone the Gordian knot, and his soldiers cheered loudly — now they knew that their king would conquer Asia.

At that time the great Persian empire was ruled by King Darius III, the great-great-grandson of the King Darius who had invaded Greece in the time of Miltiades. When Darius III heard that Alexander had undone the Gordian Knot he was determined to prove the prophecy wrong. He gathered together an immense army of six hundred thousand men and led it against Alexander's thirty thousand warriors: that is twenty Persians to every one Greek soldier. The two armies met near the city of Issus in a battle which was to decide the fate of Persia, Europe and Asia. And the year in which the famous battle of Issus took place is easily remembered; it was three hundred and thirty three years before the birth of Christ.

The Persians, as usual, put their faith in their great numbers, while the Macedonians relied on the clever generalship of Alexander and on their courage and skill with weapons. Alexander was in the thick of the battle, and he and his horsemen hacked their way towards Darius who was driving a war chariot. But when Darius III saw his enemies coming he was so frightened that he turned his horses and fled. And when the Persian soldiers saw their king running away they lost heart. Soon the whole vast Persian army was in full flight. The Macedonians captured a huge amount of treasure after the battle: King Darius' tent contained a wealth of golden vessels, silver and jewellery. And in the Persians' haste to flee, the king's mother and wife were also left behind in the tent. But Alexander treated the two women as royal guests rather than enemy prisoners.

King Darius III had fled, but when he heard how well his wife and mother were treated, he said: "O gods, if I must lose my empire give it to no one but Alexander!" So he sent messengers to Alexander to make an offer of peace. And this was his offer: he would give Alexander his daughter to marry and half the Persian kingdom, but Darius would keep the other half. Alexander turned to one of his Macedonian officers, whose name was Parmenio, and asked: "What do you think of this offer?" Parmenio said: "If I were Alexander, I would be satisfied." "So would I, if I were Parmenio," Alexander replied. But the young Macedonian king wanted all of Persia and so the war continued.

Alexander's army rested briefly after the Battle of Issus and then set out in pursuit of Darius. For several days they rode across a huge desert, and, with their water rations gone, the soldiers began to suffer an unbearable thirst. The sun burnt down with a terrible glare, their lips were dry and parched, and there was not one soldier who would not have gladly given all that he owned for a drink of water. Then a horseman came galloping up to Alexander carrying water from a distant oasis in his helmet. Alexander took the helmet and, looking round, saw the eyes of his thirsty, suffering Macedonian soldiers all watching him. "Should I be the only one to drink?" he asked. Then he turned the helmet upside down and poured the water into the sand. A great cheer went up and his men shouted: "Lead us on Alexander! With you as leader we feel neither thirst nor tiredness." The next day they reached a river where they could quench their thirst. And from that time the soldiers loved Alexander even more because he had shared their hardships and thirst.

54. The Last Battle

Darius III, the man who had once been called the King of Kings, was in retreat. And at a place called Gaugamela he fought his last battle against Alexander. But again the courage and skill of Alexander and his Macedonians brought victory. Once more Darius fled to another part of Persia. Now, the governor of this province was called Bessus, and he wanted to win favour with Alexander, so he had King Darius murdered. But when Alexander heard about it, he was furious: he had declared war on Darius and would have killed the Persian in a fair fight but he would never have murdered a defenceless man — enemy or friend. So Alexander gave the dead king a splendid royal funeral while the treacherous governor, Bessus, was condemned to death.

The cities of Persia opened their gates to the victorious Macedonians and hailed Alexander as their new king. The ancient city of Babylon surrendered without resistance. Egypt had been under Persian rule for a long time, and the Egyptians hated the Persian oppressors so they received Alexander gladly and proclaimed him their leader. And where the Nile flows into the sea, Alexander had a new city built which was called Alexandria in his honour. There, the first university was established and the wisest men of Greece, Persia, Babylon and Egypt came together to teach students the wisdom of Greece and Asia. For the next thousand years the University of Alexandria was a place of learning like no other in the world.

However, there was still one land to be conquered, and that was India. But first, Alexander and his soldiers needed time to rest and enjoy their conquests. But the faithful Macedonians were not so happy with their young king. During the war against Darius III, Alexander had shared all the hardships. But now, as the ruler of a mighty empire — Macedonia, Greece, Persia, Babylon and Egypt — Alexander lived in luxury like a

Persian king. He dressed in rich Persian robes and, if a soldier wanted to speak to the mighty Alexander, he was expected to prostrate himself on the floor before him.

The sturdy Macedonians did not like these Persian customs and many of them grumbled that Alexander had become too proud and behaved more like a Persian than a Greek. And one of those who grumbled was Clitus, the man who had saved Alexander's life in the battle at Granicus.

Now, one night, during a great banquet, Alexander's Persian courtiers praised and flattered the young king. They called him the greatest general of all times. But Clitus, who was sitting by Alexander's side, remained silent. Alexander, who had drunk too much wine, turned to Clitus and asked: "Do you not agree with what they say?"

"No," answered Clitus, "I think your father, Philip, was a better general than you are."

Alexander leapt up, red in the face with anger. The other men tried to quieten Clitus but again he said: "I have fought for King Philip. I know he was better!" Drunk and mad with fury, Alexander tore a spear from the hands of a guard and thrust it into Clitus' heart. But the next moment Alexander realized what he had done. He threw himself over the body of Clitus, he called his name, he cried bitterly, but it was too late, For three days Alexander mourned his friend. He took neither food nor drink and spent his time praying that the spirit of Clitus would forgive him.

A few months later, King Alexander announced that his army was ready to march to India, a land even larger than the Persian empire. At first the Macedonian soldiers were pleased; they would rather have the hardships and dangers of war than the luxuries of Persia which had changed their beloved king. So they marched and rode until they came to the Himalayan mountains.

Between the towering mountain peaks they found the Khyber Pass and crossed into India. There were many Indian kingdoms, but one by one they fell to the Macedonians. In one great battle they had to fight against Indian cavalry mounted on elephants. However, not long after that Alexander's soldiers

grew tired of marching and fighting. They were homesick for
the mountains of Macedonia which they had not seen for ten
years and, when they reached the middle of India, they refused
to go any further. Alexander was furious but, for once, his faithful Macedonians would not obey him. Against Alexander's will,
the army marched back to Persia. And so Alexander remained
unbeaten; the only time he had to retreat was when his own soldiers forced him to do so.

Back in Persia, Alexander began to consider new conquests,
but in the midst of his planning he caught a fever. It may have
been malaria, but no doctor could help and he became weaker
and weaker. When his Macedonian soldiers heard that the king
was dying, they hurried to the palace. They filed past his bed
and so Alexander the Great saw for the last time the brave men
who had fought with him. And the fierce warriors, who had
faced danger without flinching, cried like children as they
passed their dying king.

When the soldiers had gone and only his generals remained,
one of them asked: "Who shall be your successor?"

Alexander replied: "The worthiest," then he died. He was
thirty three years old and had left Greece only ten years before.
But in those ten years he had created an empire greater than the
world had ever seen.

But after his death this great empire fell apart. His generals
fought each other for a slice of the empire and each piece
became a separate kingdom again. But you see, in each of these
kingdoms there was now a Greek or Macedonian ruler and
Greek traders, craftsmen and teachers. And so, in one way,
Alexander's great hope and dream did come true; the swords of
his Macedonians had opened the way for Greek knowledge and
Greek art to flow into the world to meet and mix with the wisdom of other nations.

And so, for the first time in history, there was a knowledge, a
wisdom, which all nations could share. This was the achieve-
ment of Alexander the Great, the man who built a great empire
in ten years.

Index